WOMAN AT THE
EDGE OF TWO WORLDS

WOMAN AT THE
EDGE OF TWO WORLDS

THE SPIRITUAL JOURNEY OF MENOPAUSE

LYNN V. ANDREWS

Illustrations by Ginny Joyner

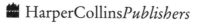

HarperCollins*Publishers*

HarperCollins books may be purchased for educational, business, or sales promotional use. For information please write: Special Markets Department, HarperCollins Publishers, Inc., 10 East 53rd Street, New York, NY 10022.

FIRST EDITION

Designed by Jessica Shatan
Illustrations © 1993 by Ginny Joyner

Library of Congress Cataloging-in-Publication Data

Andrews, Lynn V.
  Woman at the edge of two worlds : the spiritual journey of menopause / Lynn V. Andrews. — 1st ed.
      p.   cm.
    ISBN 0–06–016956–7
    1. Andrews, Lynn V. 2. Middle aged women—Religious life. 3. Aged women—Religious life. 4. Menopause—Psychological aspects. 5. Shamanism. I. Title.
BP610.A54188   1993
612.6'65—dc20   92–56215

---

93 94 95 96 97 ❖/RRD 10 9 8 7 6 5 4 3 2 1

Woman at the Edge of Two Worlds is about the fire within and the great mysteries around the passage of menopause. This book is dedicated to all my sisters who have entered this gateway and been transformed. I have dedicated each chapter to a different aspect of your sacred fire. Whether you felt the hot flash of transformation and the alchemy of fire or not, this book is dedicated to you, sacred women, the keepers of the eternal fire.

Some of the names and places in this book have been changed to protect the privacy of those involved.

The ceremonies portrayed in this book originate from the ancient history of the Sisterhood of the Shields and not from tribal customs and traditions of the Native American.

Agnes was looking at the passing water of the stream. She began to speak very quietly, "As we women are related to the water, it is good to be near moving water during your moon. We are born of the first words of the first mother. We are of the void and we carry the void. Our blood is her body. It is sacred. It is said she was born of the water and the earth, and that is why your blood shall return to the earth and your spirit to the waters of the sacred dream. Her power shall be honored over all the earth, and all men shall know her as the beginning. And now that you have transformed your body into the womb time, take care that your blood seed of our first mother is welcomed in a sacred way, for it is of her body. Her flesh has been burned that you may be given life. Her smoke will bring wisdom to your way. Smoke is a gift from the first mother's heart. Bless her memory, for she lives within you. When you eat, it is she who eats. When you smoke, it is she who takes your message to the faraway. When you bleed, it is she who bleeds. When you give your body to be divided in love, let all parts of you be in her name so that her love can be complete on this great earth."

—AGNES WHISTLING ELK
Flight of the Seventh Moon

CONTENTS

Riding the Fire

The Alchemy of Hot Flashes

Dancing the Fire

Living with Menopause

The Cauldron of Truth

After You Have Realized Menopause

Arousal of the Inner Fire

Rekindling the Heat of Earlier Menopause

PROLOGUE

POWER ANIMAL: THE FIRE IS BORN

Lashika, the she-wolf, her eyes glittering like amber flames in the darkness, curled up around her pups. They slept in a dark cave dug out of the side of a mountain by slow-moving glaciers centuries ago. Her belly was full and normally she would sleep through the long night and the day following, but carried on the high north wind was an unfamiliar sound. She raised her head, suddenly alert, listening for danger, anything that would harm the life of her small family. She was the female alpha wolf, strongest, blackest, most powerful of her kind. The rest of her pack and her mate were sleeping, curled and quiet in their dreams, but Lashika sensed something exciting in the air, something that stirred her heart and the life force of the Great Spirit that ran through every cell in her body.

Slowly, trying not to disturb her pups, she crept to the entrance of the cave. She looked up at the night sky. The waning moon was at its zenith. She sniffed the air and tasted the scent of cedar smoke. She listened. Now she was fully awake. There was singing. Every once in a while, the high north wind would bring the sounds to her of she-human voices, and then the wind would shift. She could sense a drumbeat far in the distance. Her curiosity got the best of her. She looked around in all of the four directions. Not a leaf was stirring. Occasionally, a west wind would move along the ground and ruffle the thick fur that was growing black and tinged with white around her neck, preparing her for the long winter months ahead. Stealthily, she reached out with her paws and stretched. Then she moved down the trail leading into an aspen forest where the voices seemed to be coming from.

She moved in silence at a strong gallop down a deer trail leading directly into the center of the trees. The sound of music, drums beating, and the voices of women high in song, came closer and closer as she galloped through the night under the protection of the towering trees. It was late fall and there was an unusual warmth in the air. She was excited and happy to be moving down a trail in darkness, her favorite time to hunt, to move into the unknown.

Soon the singing became quite loud and the earth pulsated with the beat of a great life drum. She moved off the deer track and into the underbrush, squatting down, still moving quickly and stealthily through the underbrush, her belly touching the ground as she moved, hardly creating a sound. She was fascinated. Her ears pricked forward, listening to every sound that came her way. She could smell the pungent scent of cedar smoke and sweetgrass. There was a light at the center of the forest, glowing like a giant sun in a midnight sky. Now she crept along underneath the brush and chokecherry bushes, the pads of her paws feeling the damp leaves beneath them, cushioning any sound that she could have made.

She pulled herself to the edge of a low ridge and looked down into the sacred circle of the Sisterhood of the Shields. She had known these women throughout her life. They had brought her great power in their ceremonies, and she had brought power to them. They had seen her occasionally on the edge of a canyon or standing atop a hill in the distance. Never had they been this close to one another, but they had honored each other in their respective rituals, each gaining respect and knowledge from the other's existence. Lashika spread her paws in front of her. She stretched her toes and gripped the earth with her claws. Enjoying the ceremony before her, she rested her head on her paws, but she was ready to spring into flight if necessary. She understood that something sacred was happening and that she was in no real danger.

A woman wearing a white doeskin beaded dress with fringe, a

red sash, and beautiful red beaded moccasins stood in the center of the circle. She was offering sacred ties, tiny medicine bundles, that represented different aspects of her life. She was giving these away to a sacred circle made out of stone before her. Within that circle were prayer sticks, four shields, and baskets. Lashika could not see the contents of the baskets; some appeared to be filled with food, human food of some kind. There were many women gathered. These women were elders. They were grandmothers. Occasionally, the fire would spit into the air, sending sparks in a spiraling action on a gust of wind. Then the faces of the women would be illuminated, their ancient brown skin tanned from the sun, the lines of time and life experience etched into their faces. Lashika was curious about their eyes. She always looked into the eyes of the beings that she met, and she read their age, their abilities, their power, their fear. She saw no fear in these eyes, but a power that she had not seen in other human faces that she had encountered in her life. She understood their vision. It was almost as if they could speak the same language. It was the language of the wilderness, the understanding of the primordial balance of nature and survival of the fittest in a world of untamed beauty. She sighed deeply, not fully understanding the depth of her perception.

The women did a slow dance in a circle for a long time. The one woman dressed in white in the center continued to pray at the altar in the sacred circle. She must be the alpha woman, Lashika thought to herself. She sniffed the air again in recognition of another powerful female in her midst. If she were to move into a position of combat, protection of her young, this would be the human she would have to fight. She knew inside herself that she would win. Lashika was born to be the leader of the pack and never once in her life had she wavered from the understanding of her own power. She looked at this woman performing a ritual here with her prayer sticks and the dancing fire as the song of the women's voices and the drumming came somewhere from the shadows around the circle, and Lashika honored her. She felt compassion, if that were possible, like she felt for her pups. There was a heartfelt connection to this woman. Slowly, the woman turned from her ceremony and looked toward Lashika. She searched the darkness, feeling the predatory eyes of the she-wolf, her power animal in the spirit world. She felt the support and the acknowledgment; if not in the physical world, she felt it in spirit.

She turned again as two women raised an elk skin above their heads. The women had long gray braids that reached to their waists. They were dressed in beautiful bright colors from another land, red and pink embroidered *huipiles* and long yellow and blue woven skirts. The tiny threads shone like a parade of fire-flies in the yellow light. They were women from nations south of the continent on which they stood. The woman in white doeskin bent low, dancing to the rhythms, and walked beneath the elk skin. She was crying now. She forgot the sense of the wolf and her presence. She forgot everything that was around her, and she grieved for the passing of life as she had known it. She grieved for the passing of her fertility, her ability to have children. She cried and wailed to the waning moon and knew, as Lashika sensed, that her life was changed forever. This was not a tragic passing or a passing of dishonor, but a passage into a new world on the other side of the elk skin. She was now a woman of wise-blood. The women gathered around her, dancing with a wild abandon. They threw something from their fingers that created sparks in the air, and they laughed and they cried and they held one another in the celebration of their birth into the new goddess life.

Lashika lifted her head and cocked it to one side. She recognized the energy coming from these women. It was not unlike the energy coming from her own wolf pack when they honored her as the leader. Like the woman, she was the one who went down the paths of life and returned to give the others strength and knowledge and wisdom. She was honored. She understood this woman somehow. She respected her from the depth of her being, and she lent her spirit to their dance.

Lashika knew that she had to return to her wolf den and her pups. She could feel a stirring in her belly; she knew that they were missing her. Very quietly she honored the circle that she had witnessed. She lifted her head to the sky, took a long, deep breath of the sacred smoke, and then she turned and stealthily moved through the undergrowth. The moon was now very low in the sky and an eerie light was on the horizon. It was the hour of the wolf, the time that Lashika knew best. She crept away from the ceremony, her feet touching the earth lightly with each beat of the drum. She raised up into a gallop, her powerful haunches striding through the darkness, leading her home. Her heart was full for her sister-being. She had witnessed the birth of a new kind of existence and life force. It was the birth of a teacher into the world of wisdom. It was the birth of a sister-being in spirit, who, not unlike herself, moved with courage into the world, gathering the knowledge that she found every day, bringing it home to her brothers and sisters so that they may live in harmony and sacred balance on Mother Earth.

Lashika paused at the top of a hill. Throwing her great head back, she closed her eyes to the shine of the moon and uttered a cry from the depths of her spirit. Her wolf song was for the beauty in life and called out for a sisterhood between all female beings. Lashika's voice echoed through the mountains long after she was gone.

INTRODUCTION

This is a book about menopause and spirituality, about the uses of the energy that a woman possesses and how she can use this energy in relation to her universe and to the spiritual and sacred aspect of her being. The issue of menopause has always been salient, but today, as we women of the baby boom reach this momentous juncture in our lives, the subject's significance reaches epic proportion.

I personally have had the good fortune of making this difficult passage under the guidance of my own teachers, the Native American elders, Agnes Whistling Elk and Ruby Plenty Chiefs. For those of you unfamiliar with my previous work with these women, I'll take a moment to explain that many years ago I was led to Agnes and Ruby by a spiritual force too powerful to resist. Since our first prodigious meeting these women and their spiritual sisters, all members of an ancient circle called the Sisterhood of the Shields, have shared with me a great wisdom which they hold in their hearts and in their minds. In turn I have communicated, at their request, their wise teachings through my books, seminars, and private work with my apprentices.

Women the world over are struggling to understand the true meaning, the essence, of their lives. I have experienced with my teachers that menopause is the gateway into the most sacred time of a woman's existence on earth, a time when she can at last discover the deeper meanings she has sought. And yet, this rite of passage is usually silent, an unspoken of and mysterious journey. We joke about our hot flashes in an attempt to make them less frightening. We have no idea that these symptoms of shifting hormones are also the kindling of a fire within that prepares a woman for an incredibly powerful time of life. As we approach this new threshold, it has been shown to me that the alchemy of heat is present to clarify the body and spirit of negative debris. Hot flashes need to be welcomed instead of fought against. So when you take part in this experience, dance with the heat and ride it like a fractious horse, knowing that there is something going on that is far more important than the physical rebalancing of hormones and the transformations taking place in your body.

The change of life is a time of release when a woman begins to reap the benefits of all that she has learned and done. It is the time when her spiritual life at last truly begins. Menopause is a process of rebirth from which a woman emerges with new responsibilities, new mirrors, and new power. At its nucleus is the discovery by each woman of her own personal mystery, an illumination of her private relationship to the totality of her own life process. As she develops, she begins to choreograph the energies of the universe in a very new way.

Every woman experiences and expresses this new understanding of self and sacredness differently. In the old way, taught to me by Agnes and Ruby, this experience can be profoundly strengthening and full of joy. To ensure such a positive effect, this particular rite of passage in a woman's life needs to be fully illuminated so that the actual event of menopause becomes, not the inevitable onset of aging and decline, but the access to the beginning of a new, beautiful way of life.

Women of today have earned positions of importance in politics and in the workplace. It is more commonly acknowledged that we are regularly required to be all things to all people. Nevertheless, though we are taking power in so many ways, there is still a residual feeling that with age women are no longer beautiful. The pernicious notion remains that as we age we become ugly. As a result women often believe they will lose their turf to younger, prettier women, that when their external beauty wanes, they will lose their power. If we don't change the way we perceive the deeper meaning of life, this assumption will continue to be, at least partially, true. In the recesses of our minds, we hold an image of an old woman stirring a cauldron—the sorceress. In ancient times that being was considered beautiful. She was an enchantress, the purveyor of magic, the giver of new life in a spiritual and a sacred sense. With the evolution of society and time, however, we have lost that image of the beautiful sorceress. Now we see her as an ugly old witch, a crone with a wart on her nose, standing over a bubbling pot of darkness, totally devoid of beauty.

As you learn the old way taught by the Sisterhood of the Shields, you will be reintroduced to the deep, internal beauty that comes with age—the beauty that makes itself visible by virtue of its innate power. As you feel this beauty, you will express it, and all those with whom you come in contact will be touched by your newfound strength, your heightened awareness, and the loveliness that emanates from deep within you.

With the invention of the Gutenberg press, the purpose and position of the elder person in society changed forever. Since the advent of typesetting there has no longer been the need for stories told by firelight long into the night. There are no more tales wisely imparted by the grandmothers and grandfathers of the village who had lived through the history their descendants yearned to hear about. Once the grandparents were valuable; they held positions of respect. Now that has all been altered. There is little left of villages and the oral tradition of bards, elders, and twisted-hairs to teach the young through performance, shamanism, and wise tales. Today we go to the library and read about our history, or we switch on the television and watch events restaged before our eyes. So the position of "who holds the knowledge" has been lost for all time, except in certain unique societies in which the ancient ways of telling are retained. In a society of this kind, the one-who-knows-how, an old man or woman, is still the most powerful individual, the wisest and most respected of its members. And traditionally, the wisest of all are the ones—the women—who hold their power and their blood. They are the women of wise-blood, the women who have gone through menopause.

Shamanism and the ancient ways of woman are as applicable to twentieth-century life as they were to the lives of native tribes 6,000 years ago. Shamanism is a way of understanding energy. Since it is not a belief structure, it doesn't interfere with an individual's personal faith. It doesn't matter, then, if you are Jewish, Christian, Buddhist, or whatever. Shamanism is a way of finding your own inner truth and light and developing the ability to manifest this power back into the world.

Woman at the Edge of Two Worlds is an archetype, a goddess figure who stands at the gateway between the first world—the first ring of power in a woman's life—and the second world. The first world is dedicated to physical existence: the raising of a family, acts of power that have to do with career, choices in relationships, and dealings with conditioning of family and society. At the second ring of power—the second world into which a woman is initiated by Woman at the Edge of Two Worlds—the great goddess provides a bridge for a woman's voyage to the enlightened, sacred life that marks the second half of her evolution.

This book is also about my own intimate experience with menopause. In it I will tell you how my teachers led me on a sacred and enlightening journey, and about how I in turn have been able to assist and guide others through this process.

It is important for the reader to understand that everyone I work with is dear to me; and further, that not everyone needs to be worked with in the same way. Each of us is unique. Every individual needs different mirrors to facilitate growth. One apprentice may need to be touched only fleetingly, as a butterfly touches a flower. In such cases the drama may even be addictive, and because of this, involved ceremony may be entirely inappropriate. Another person may require greater attention and continual support, while yet another may have variable needs.

In this book I work with four of my women apprentices in Los Angeles who are experiencing menopause in very diverse ways. Together we build new ways of empowering our lives and the lives of our families through new spiritual integration with our everyday world. Our energy fields often become polluted, and so it is my custom to join with the Sisterhood in cleansing the energy field of an apprentice whenever this is appropriate. Needless to say, I would never invade a person's privacy by undertaking such a procedure without express consent; and because of the very personal nature of this cleansing, I have never before revealed exactly how it is done. But I think that now is the right time to do so.

Don't be afraid of a new idea like shamanism. It really is only a word that describes a way to live in balance with one foot in the world of physical everyday existence, and a foot in a healthy spiritual life. Shamanism does not require you to believe in anything but yourself.

Many women never progress beyond the first lesson of power—that we are alone. I demonstrate through my own life process and interactions with my teachers and apprentices that we need not fear this circumstance because the last lesson of power is that we are truly all one. Menopause creates an innate feeling of isolation and separateness in many of us. It is a passage we experience all alone. It is my fervent hope that through these teachings I can give you a place to turn when you think you have none—a way through a seemingly impenetrable maze. I want you to be able to find answers to the questions you can't verbalize.

This book will show how I chose another path and how you can do the same. I have learned that the moment the change of life begins is the point at which true sisterhood with other women is born.

It was the "hour of the wolf," just before dawn. In my sleep I felt a cool breeze on my cheek, and I heard the call of the elk whistling, high-pitched and haunting, in the semidarkness of my dreaming. I recognized the summons from Agnes to join her in the spirit world—that shadowy realm of astral flight into which we fly with our energy forms, all white and blue mist surrounded by occasional flashes of yellow light. Guided by my intent, we traveled to the domain of my apprentice, Sara, who had sought our cleansing power. She was asleep below us, her astral form hovering above, her body shimmering in a lavender and gray shadow. As if swimming beneath a coral reef with odd shapes occasionally floating by and opaque, iridescent sheets of light moving in and out of view, Agnes and I went to work. She placed herself across from me, and with the strength of our wills, we cleaned dark spots out of Sara's energy field by shooting a flow of power and light back and forth between us until the spots were gone. We only left when they were replaced by soft green light manifested from our hearts.

The next day Sara came to me. A beautiful woman, Sara sat across from me in my living room in Los Angeles. It was a cool November day and a warm fire cast flickering shadows of gold across her high cheekbones.

"I'm a lawyer, Lynn, and somehow the years got away from me. I'm in menopause and never had the child that I wanted," Sara said, tears running down her cheeks.

"Perhaps, Sara, I can share with you another kind of birth—a sacred child that is waiting to be born."

"What do you mean?" she asked, an interested glow lighting her eyes.

"That sacred child could be your own spirit reborn. This is the beginning of a new time for you—the spiritual time of your life."

We did a drumming ceremony together. Then we went to work to prepare her for her initiation with Woman at the Edge of Two Worlds.

GATHERING THE WOOD

THE SEARCH FOR KNOWLEDGE
WHAT'S HAPPENING TO YOUR BODY?

Woman at the Edge of Two Worlds stood before me in my cave of initiation.

"I am the fire," she said, her face glowing. "I can only move upward as I burn. You, my daughter, are apprenticed to the fire. Whether you dreamed of the vast possibility of transformation or not, your body is now your teacher. Feel the burn of the heat and welcome the fire, for the fire is I, the goddess woman who changes you and prepares you for your sacred life. Gather knowledge about yourself and your body. This knowledge is the wood for your central flame."

I

DENIAL OF THE FIRE

I've always thought of sporting events like horse shows as being tiny microcosms of life, taking form and presenting an entire lifetime of struggle and experience in a single day or two. This particular horse show was no different.

"Pam, will you please give me a leg up?" I asked of my horse trainer.

"Look, girl, if you can't get on, you can't ride."

Pam was tense and her Southern drawl irritated me. I was struggling to get on my horse. It had been raining, and I had my chaps rolled up halfway to the knee so that they wouldn't get dirty in the muddy ring before my class. I teetered around, hopping backward and forward on one foot, trying to get my leg up high enough so that I could get my toe into the stirrup of my Western saddle.

"Lynn, what *is* the matter?" Pam grumbled again, impatiently, checking her watch.

"I don't know what it is, Pam. The cleaners must have shrunk these pants. They've never been tight like this. I'm afraid that I'm going to rip them right down the middle."

"Come on, Lynn," Pam urged again, "you've got a class to ride. We don't have all day, you know."

Droplets of perspiration were beginning to bead on my upper lip. Sweat was getting into my eyes and stinging my eyelids. Finally, with a groan I got my foot into the stirrup and vaulted up onto the back of Magic Lady, my lovely mare, who stood spraddle-legged against my sudden movement. Her nostrils flared in expectation of the coming class. Her neck was arched like a swan as I adjusted the reins. She was groomed to perfection and her bay coat glistened in the artificial light from the arena beacons overhead.

Pam grabbed hold of my leg and shook my knee. "Come on now, Lynn, get your act together. For God's sake, why are you sweating so? You're going to float right off this horse."

She threw me a towel and I began to dab at my face. Realizing that my makeup was coming off onto the towel, I threw it back to her.

"Look, Pam, I don't know what's the matter with me. Maybe I'm just nervous, but get off my back, will you." Tears began to well up in my eyes.

"Oh, for heaven's sake, don't tell me you're going to cry," Pam said, scuffing her toe in the dirt. She was a tough cowgirl and tolerated no show of emotion. I took my horses very seriously and was usually totally under control. My behavior and weakness was throwing her as much as it was me. Taking a rag, she wiped off my boots and spurs and rolled down my chaps giving my legs a longer look.

"I could use a little support, you know," I said, hoping that I wasn't going to start blubbering before I had to ride into the ring.

"Come on, Lynn, I'm sorry. It's just unusual to see you so unstrung. It makes me nervous," Pam said.

"Likewise," I answered. "I'm sorry, Pam," I mumbled as we headed toward the gate.

Other riders thronged into the covered passageway leading into the arena, everyone nervous, wearing brightly colored Western outfits and tight little smiles. Suddenly I was struck by the fact that they were all so young. Most of the girls I was riding against were in their early twenties. I laughed to myself as I wiped the perspiration on my lip carefully with the back of my gloved hand, leaving a slight stain from the wetness. Damn, I thought, why am I so hot? I had been riding in horse shows for years and this had never happened to me.

We were quickly guided by the damp cement walls of the dark corridor into white blazing lights. I heard the cheers of a throng of onlookers in the large open space of the show arena, which was hung with multicolored flags. As I rode into the ring, my heart began to palpitate. I could see that my mare was concerned. I was not riding with my usual confidence. She flicked her ears back and forth, trying to get a reading on this rider who seemed to be behaving so differently than usual.

"Jog your horses," the announcer blared in my ear. His voice seemed unnaturally loud over the organ music. Magic Lady moved ahead in perfect position as we wove in and out of traffic. I could tell that the judge was watching me. She was a tall, thin woman from Oklahoma. I could see that she had written my number down on her pad as I made a beautiful pass around her. Again, tears welled up in my eyes for no reason. I couldn't imagine what was wrong with me. This time they were tears of extreme joy, as if I had just won the Olympics. My hand was trembling slightly, and again, my mare flicked her ears in obvious concern. When the announcer asked for a canter, we moved easily into the gait. We loped around the covered arena, and I thought for a moment about an old saying by Benjamin Disraeli that "a good canter is the cure for all evil." I started to laugh to myself as I rode by Pam on the rail. She looked at me in shock, because I was actually laughing. I could hear Pam hissing between her teeth, "Lynn, for Christ's sake, concentrate on what you're doing."

The next thing I knew, we were lining up in the center of the ring, all thirty-eight of us, one lovely nubile face after another, and then me, sitting astride my horse, sopping wet. Again and again I dabbed my lip, hoping that my lipstick wasn't running down my neck and into my shirt. As I rode out of the ring with my third-place ribbon, Magic Lady, my young mare, sidestepped nervously as I reached the out gate. Pam met me, took my horse's reins, and led me off to the side. By now, I was in tears again. Pam handed me a tissue.

"Blow your nose. For heaven's sake, Lynn. I didn't mean to hurt your feelings. I'm really sorry. I was just nervous."

Now I was really crying. "I'm sorry, Pam. I don't know what is the matter with me. I guess I just needed more sleep or something."

My tears were mostly from confusion. My reactions were not familiar to me. Lurking in the back of my mind was the thought that maybe I was having some kind of nervous breakdown.

"I guess I have been under a lot of stress," I remarked as I got off my horse. Magic Lady looked around at me as if to say, What's the matter, Mom? She nudged my arm with her nose, looking for carrots. I followed her and Pam back to the barn, blotting at my eyes, tears running down my cheeks. Several arms reached out as I passed various other trainers. They patted me on the back, thinking that my tears were because I had gotten a third place. "Better luck next time, Lynn. Can't win 'em all," somebody yelled. I laughed tearfully, wanting just to get out of there and hide.

As I peeled off my clothes in the dressing room, I realized with amazement that they were soaked through. It was a cool day out. I shook my head and finally stood in front of the mirror and looked at myself in wonderment. I toweled off my body as if I'd been in a shower.

"Maybe I should call my doctor," I said to myself. "I haven't been in for a check-up in a long time." I made a mental note to make arrangements to see him in the next few days.

The face looking back at me in the mirror was somebody I didn't recognize. My eyes were red. My face had changed. It wasn't so much that I had aged in the last few years, but that the actual shape of my face had changed. I didn't look like the same person that I had been all these years. I sat down on a stool, still staring at my reflection, and I realized that I didn't feel exactly the same either. My body, in some senses, was more acutely aware of the rhythms of nature around me than it had ever been. I felt things more deeply than I ever had, emotionally. I had a sense of people's anger and emotions and tension more than I ever had, as well as their joy. When I felt those rhythms pervading my own body, it would bring tears to my eyes. I felt emotionally involved with the world, as if I were riding the moon through her phases from one end of my life to the other. My perceptions seemed different. Colors seemed brighter. Everything was accentuated. I laughed to myself, "Right, it's called overly sensitive, Lynn."

The next morning I awoke in my home in Los Angeles. I felt wonderful, and it seemed like the day before at the horse show had been a bad dream. My spirits were high. I felt serene as I brushed my hair, the sun streaming in from the high windows in my bedroom. I meditated for a while and then did the shaman dance of power in my backyard. The movements resemble Tai Chi. As I lifted my arms under the lemon tree and felt the rhythms and cadence of nature entering my fingers, I felt centered and strong again. I heard my teacher Agnes Whistling Elk's voice in my head. "Walk in balance, my daughter, with a foot in spirit and a foot in the physical world of manifestation. Always live from your center." I knew I would see Agnes very soon.

An hour later when I entered the house, I picked up the phone and dialed my mother's phone number. Her cheerful, sweet voice said, "Hello."

"Hi, Mom," I said, so grateful as always to hear her voice.

"How did you do in the show, honey?"

"I only placed third," I said. "It was a very strange day. I don't know what happened to me; I just kind of lost it. I guess I was nervous."

"What happened?"

"Well, I seem to be very puffy and gaining weight lately. I don't know why. My pants were too tight, and Pam and I were out of sync."

"You look awfully thin to me," she said.

"Well, I seem to be retaining water, and I don't know what happens to me lately, Mom. I'm really emotional, I guess, or nervous."

"Oh, honey, you're under just too much stress. You're working too hard. Maybe you need a vacation."

"Good idea, Mom, maybe we can go somewhere."

"Oh, goody," she said, with a smile in her voice.

"Mom, what are you going to do today?"

"I'm going off to the lawyer's," she said, "to finish my will." Vanessa, my daughter, was driving her there.

"Okay, just be careful, will you? I don't know what I would do if anything ever happened to you."

"Oh, don't worry, sweetheart. I'm just fine."

There was a hesitation in my mother's voice that betrayed her cheerfulness.

"Mom, what is it that's on your mind?"

"Oh, nothing," she said.

"No, really, Mama, what is the matter?"

"Oh, I'm just worried about money, but I don't want you to concern yourself with it. You have your own money problems."

"Of course I'm concerned, Mom. Just figure out what your bills are and I'll help you take care of it. Just let me know."

"All right," she said, as she sighed with relief. She would never ask anyone for anything. It was just her way. She would keep a stiff upper lip and go out into her daily routine with a smile and a bright, shining face and move through her life as if she hadn't a care in the world. But I was concerned about her. She had lost her husband, Jim, my wonderful stepfather, a year before, and I knew that she felt lonely. That's why my twenty-one-year-old daughter was living with her. Even so, Mom was eighty-two years old, and anything could happen to her.

"And darling, what are you going to do today?" she finally asked.

"Well, I have to work all day, but I'm going to meet a friend for lunch, and then I'll be back at the house writing. So when you get back, just let me know how it went at the lawyer's."

We said good-bye with happiness and the usual sense of well-being and affection. It was the last time I would ever speak to my mother alive.

2

DEATH AND REBIRTH OF THE FIRE

I sat next to my mother on my birthday weekend, counting her breaths and scanning the vivid graph lines on the machines in intensive care. My own body was flaming hot and cold, with flashes of heat almost in rhythm with her breaths. My heart was beating with her heart, echoing a passage of mystery so many years ago when she had introduced me into the physical world. I cried then as I cried now, with bewilderment at the force of nature and the terror of separation. No longer were these the buoyant meanderings of a soul cresting the tide of an effortless existence. My mind was twisting and turning like a whale deep beneath the surface of the sea. The lessons to be learned were surfacing as they had at my birth. When someone dies, I have always felt that a part of each of us goes with them. When a new child is born, I feel that a part of each and every one of us is given new life.

I felt the soft, sweet skin of Mother's hand beneath my fingers. She seemed so tiny and innocent, much as I must have felt to her when I was born. I remembered she had told me it was snowing that March day in Seattle. I looked out the window of the hospital in Los Angeles. I was stunned to see a gathering of black storm clouds hovering over Westwood as it began to snow. Mother's breathing became shallow and the neon graph lines began to straighten. I knew she was nearing release. Outside, the sky had become strangely red and violet and then slowly became a brilliant yellow. A sudden beam of golden light filled the room, and Mother opened her blue-gray eyes from her coma one last time. She looked up toward the light and then closed her eyes again to explore her inner vision that I could never know. A slight smile lit up her pale face. It had stopped snowing, and the sky was graced by a huge double rainbow over the city. That was all, but it was enough for me. She had found peace.

After this experience and the weeks of mourning, I spent many hours in the desert with Agnes Whistling Elk.

"This desert is like death," Agnes said, running the palm of her brown hand over the red sand.

"How is that, Agnes?"

"It is immense with its own kind of beauty and undisturbed peacefulness."

"I want to believe that my mother has found a place of such beauty," I said, unable to stop the tears.

"A desert is full of distance. Distance is a god, just like your mother is a god."

Agnes drew a tiny pyramid in the sand with her fingers.

"I don't understand," I said.

"Is your mother not full of beauty? She goes on forever, like the distance—there is no end. There are no boundaries to this silence and distance that we see here in the desert. Perhaps it goes on forever, undisturbed, eternal." Agnes squinted at me, her eyes shining like polished mirrors beneath her wrinkled lids.

"I have an immense longing to see her again," I said.

"Let the winds of power pervade your being, my child. Let the wind force of all that has gone before blow through you and soothe your aching heart. Your mother no longer resides on this earth. But rebirth and transformation have occurred, and your mother lives on in the cosmic soul of the Great Spirit."

A gentle wind from the south had come up and spiraled the sand into a tiny funnel in front of us.

"See," said Agnes. "It is a sign. The sacred dance of life and time is brought to us on the wind. The essence of your mother's joy dances before you. She has shed her body like a suit of clothes. Take this moment and find true communication in the silence. Listen to the birds in their song and the words of your mother. Do not force your stillness, but let it emanate from the quiet of your perfect heart."

We sat in stillness for a long time. My eyes were closed, but I could feel the tiny twister circling around us. Occasionally, the wind would whistle as it blew through the Joshua trees. Finally, a great joy welled up inside me, and I was no longer aware of a separation between me and Agnes or the land. The wind had carried me into its song. As it circled about me in an ever rising tumultuousness, I stayed quiet like a stone in the midst of a sand storm.

Then I heard Mother's soft voice.

My daughter, the gateway to death is a strange gateway. The will of the Great Spirit is the only power that allows passage. As I once gave you birth, as once you were inside me, now you give birth to me, as I am forever within you.

3

THE END OF DENIAL

The next afternoon Agnes Whistling Elk and I sat on a mesa top in a southern California desert. Agnes's skin, darkly tanned from the sun, looked rich and velvety brown against her silver and turquoise necklace. She wore a brightly colored Guatemalan skirt and blouse given to her by Zoila, one of the women of the Sisterhood. Her shiny gray hair was pulled back in a knot at the nape of her neck. I wore jeans and a white cotton shirt. Together we looked out across the vast expanse of wilderness desert, down across the border of Mexico and into the Baja wilderness.

"Agnes, I don't understand what is happening to me. It is like my emotions have become an entity unto themselves."

Agnes smiled as she listened, the sun twinkling golden in her eyes.

"My emotions have a life of their own; they're taking me over. They're almost adversarial," I said, poking the ground with a stick.

I felt my body flush with a jolt of heat. It was a cool afternoon, but unusually temperate for early spring in the desert. Agnes placed the back of her hand against my forehead and giggled to herself, folded her hands neatly in her lap, and just watched me like an owl watches its prey scurrying in and out of its hole. I was getting uncomfortable with her stare. Finally, I looked at her square in the eye.

"Well, what is it?" I asked, dabbing my upper lip and forehead with a tissue, and then my neck. I was extraordinarily hot. It was as if I were sitting on a beach in the middle of summer.

After several minutes Agnes finally, chuckling to herself, said very quietly, "My daughter, when are you going to admit it?"

"What do you mean, 'it'?" I asked, now feeling quite unable to look her in the eye.

"When are you going to face what's happening to you?"

"I don't know what you're talking about."

Agnes threw her head back and laughed uproariously, hands together. She took her mother rattle out of one of her medicine bundles and began shaking the rattle in a ring around my head, forming a halo of sound. The mother rattle was always hypnotic to me. I closed my eyes and took a deep breath, as tears began to roll down my cheeks. The mother rattle always reminded me of my own mother. I sat in the center of a circle of sacred sound, the crystals within the gourd rattle sounding like water over a fall. The sound caressed my sensibilities, and I found myself releasing emotion that I had pent up for weeks. The grief that I was experiencing over my mother's death was devastating and was shaking me to my very foundations.

"I'm not thinking clearly," I said to Agnes. When I finally opened my eyes, she rested the rattle in my lap.

"When someone you love passes on," Agnes said, "it leaves a big, empty canyon in your heart."

"It's so strange," I answered. "I know that Mother is in a wonderful place now. I know that she's with the Great Spirit and with her husband and that Mother is free from the tremendous stress that she felt in this lifetime. But I am left behind, and my life has changed so much, and I feel her absence, it seems, every moment."

"Lynn, it is time," she said very gruffly, turning from a kind, ancient face full of merriment and understanding to a woman of power who sat next to me like a bolt of lightning, energy radiating off her body and filling me with strength.

I looked at her, and suddenly I realized that I had been in denial for months. "It's true, isn't it," I said. "I'm actually going through menopause, aren't I?"

"Yes, my daughter, it is time that you enter this new sacred lodge. It is time. We must do ceremony soon."

"But my mother never talked about the change of life," I said defensively.

"But your mother had a hysterectomy when she was in her late thirties, did she not?" Agnes said.

"That's correct, and she told me that she never had hot flashes; she never had anything. She just breezed right through it. She never took estrogen or progesterone or anything," I said, feeling like a child and wishing I were still a child. My images of menopause were of women going crazy. No matter what my teachings had been about the sacred passage of menopause, my mind seemed to have reverted to old conditioning. I had been told for years by various friends of mine who were older that oftentimes people are hospitalized when they go through the change of life because of the imbalance of hormones. I really didn't want to think about that. I felt crazy enough as it was with the grief that I was feeling.

"Lynn, you are a true woman of power. I can't believe you're acting like this. This gateway presents a great honor for any woman, and you know this." Agnes reached out her hand and placed it on my shoulder. This time her smile was very kind and understanding. "You are going through tremendous grief. You have lost many of the people in your family. It is not an easy time, so you may as well deal with your own physical body, because what is the physical body, but a mirror for your spirit. You are at a plateau; you have been at a plateau for some time. Menopause is a rite of passage. It is the time for moving fully and at last into your sacred life."

"It sounds like I'm being sent to a monastery," I said.

Agnes laughed and simply watched me from that extraordinary position of power within her. Suddenly I was overwhelmed with gratefulness for a teacher like her. "Agnes, thank God you are with me. I don't know what I would do if you were not in my life. Maybe all my grief has made me half crazy. I don't know why I'm in such denial. I know this is a highly important time, but I don't feel ready. Please help me. Tell me about the old way, Agnes. Tell me how the change of life was different then for women."

Agnes took a deep breath and rocked back and closed her eyes with a wistful smile. For many moments I simply watched the shift of light shimmering down from the clouds, moving across our bodies and the mesa like leaves of light in the wind.

"It was so different then," she began. "The balance on our great mother," Agnes touched the red earth with the palms of her hands, "was very, very different. In the days that I speak of there was a matriarch on the earth. That is not to say that it was a better time or a worse time; it was simply different. The matriarch had problems too. But in those days men followed the woman's line. They took the woman's name in marriage. Money, or what was considered money, followed the woman's line. Clay pots and baskets were a great source of wealth. They represented the sacred void that woman carries. As I told you long ago, in those days woman was born pregnant and man was to be impregnated by woman. That was how people approached life; that was the point of view. Everything was celebrated by a rite of passage, whether a boy child or a girl child, and as the growth process occurred, there was always a ceremony when puberty was attained, for pregnancy, for birth, for accomplishments in spiritual life. There were so many fewer people on the earth, and it was an abundant earth. The people did not destroy to live. Whatever was taken was a sacred giveaway back to the spirit that gave us life.

"When a woman went through the change of life, it was the most sacred transition. In times gone by when women were no longer fertile, they were thrown away by the societies they lived in, because they could no longer bear children. They were no longer of use. In the old, old way people did not die at age forty-five or fifty, which was the life expectancy of women at just the turn of the last century. We lived to be very old. The serenity in life was great. There was not the stress of twentieth-century living. We knew how to use the herbs and the bark of the trees. There were many herbs that replaced estrogen and progesterone and testosterone in the human body, and we used them well then. Many of those plants are extinct now, but a few still survive in what is left of the rain forests. I have tried to save some, and I will introduce you to those. There are Chinese herbs now that we do not have on this continent. I will tell you about them later, but first of all, my daughter, I want you to know that there was a time on this earth that was very, very sacred for all women, and it was not a time of control or manipulation. It was simply a sacred time.

"At the change of life came the highest initiation that you would live through as a woman—it was your initiation into your sacred and spiritual world. Younger women were not allowed into these ceremonies, nor were they allowed into the sacred caves that held the knowledge. Those caves were called by different names around the world, but I will speak of what I know. At the entrance to these caves—some of which are in the Dreamtime, some of which are in the physical lodge of reality—there were sacred guardians, keepers of the caves. The guardian that you will meet, that you will become familiar with, is Woman at the Edge of Two Worlds. She is the goddess who initiates all women into their sacredness. She takes you through the labyrinths of mystery and change as you become Changing Woman and helps you to discover the highest plateaus of consciousness. These initiations have been forgotten, because the patriarch has become so strong in our existence.

"You are about to embark on the most important part of your life. To become lost in terror about bone loss and heart disease and cancer and aging is to lose what this time can teach you. I understand your fear, because it is real. You need to comfort your body; you need to help your body understand what is happening. When you have been fed a certain food for years and you suddenly take that food away, like estrogen, you need to replace it with something equally as powerful. But your state of mind is the most important thing. It is important that you do not throw away your life and say to yourself that you have no more reason to be alive. That would be a tragedy.

"I know that you have been in denial. I know that you have been afraid of what's happening to you. It was almost easier for you to think that you were having a nervous breakdown than estrogen depletion. I understand. Because you were in extraordinary grief, and even though you still are, the time has come for your initiation to begin. When you have experienced the ceremony that the Sisterhood has prepared for you, you will then be able to take what you have learned back to your people, who so desperately need to walk in balance, with one foot in the physical and one foot in spirit. They have lost their spiritual understanding, they have lost their sacred vision, and so many of your people have lost their spirit. But you will help lead your sisters back to the source of their own truth."

I put my arms around my teacher. She held me close for a long time. The sun set on the horizon, filling the sky with orange and purple and pink, and the clouds above were edged in gold as the desert prepared for night, the sands turning purple and the Joshua trees standing like quiet sentinels, guardians of the desert floor.

4

DISILLUSIONMENT

Before Agnes and I parted company, she told me that if I was to be as much help to my menopausal sisters as I could be, I needed to experience, firsthand, the treatment women regularly receive from the modern medical community. So, obedient to the end, I made the appointment every woman dreads regardless of her age or condition, and a few days later, I headed for my gynecologist's office. As I drove along the freeway, I let my mind wander, and I was soon listening in on an imaginary conversation.

"Great news, Lynn," said the imaginary doctor. "The FDA has just approved an all natural antiaging drug that reverses the effects of menopause!"

"Terrific! How soon can we start the treatment?"

"Right away," he said, "but let me finish. Here's the best part. This stuff is also an anticarcinogenic, which means that you'll never need to have another pelvic or pap smear as long as you live!"

Moments later I was unceremoniously jerked back to reality when I nearly knocked my teeth out on the steering wheel. In my meanderings, I'd managed to forget about the speed bump that had been placed at the entrance to the doctor's parking lot. I found a parking place and made my way to my doctor's office.

I entered the office and blinked my eyes, attempting to refocus in the dimly lit room. An opaque dimpled glass slider shot open and a wide-eyed woman in pale blue polyester asked, "Yes?"

"Lynn Andrews," I said, mimicking her cryptic manner.

"It will be just a few minutes." And the dimpled glass shot shut with a whooshing sound.

I felt nervous and apprehensive as I sat on the hard leather sofa, but I had "symptoms" I had to discuss. I didn't want to hear about my menopause and its physical consequences. All I wanted was to meet Woman at the Edge of Two Worlds so I could understand in a spiritual way what was happening to me. I looked around the darkened foyer full of neon sculptures and fish tanks bubbling with South American killer fish with iridescent blue, yellow, and green sides and bulging eyes. They swam back and forth searching for food with mouths often gaping open in a look of incredulity, looking not unlike how I felt.

A sliding wooden panel door highly polished with lemon Pledge squeaked open, and Dr. Thoms peered into the semidarkness, trying to see me. "Andrews, you're next," my long-time doctor said as he ushered me into the examination room. "And where have you been? I've missed you."

"I've had a lot on my mind," I mumbled softly as he flung a paper sheet at me.

"Are you all right?" he asked.

"Yes," I lied, "why?"

"You are acting very different, dolly," he said. Then, as though he suddenly remembered some incredibly important appointment, he seemed to shift gears from the friendly family doctor to the brusque, overly busy specialist. "I'll be right back," he said curtly, "and please hurry, Lynn. We're really stacked up."

Another sliding door whooshed shut, and I stood there clutching my sheet for several minutes. Then I disrobed quickly and attempted to cover myself with a flimsy paper garment, trying to maintain a modicum of dignity. I slid awkwardly up onto the newly papered table, the empty chrome stirrups staring at my face. I stared back at them and a montage of pictures fleeted through my mind. For some reason I saw my teacher, Ruby, being raped by white surveyors and then blinded by their compass points so she could not identify them. I thought of my mother having a hysterectomy too soon in life and for no real reason. My old roommate and her horrifying abortion in Tijuana after which she nearly died from loss of blood all illuminated in my head in living color along with the glorious birth of my daughter. I was not in great shape for what happened next.

Dr. Thoms burst into the room, grabbed his rubber gloves, and shut the slider after his polyester clad assistant. She was not familiar to me and seemed very cold and abrupt. Dr. Thoms placed my bare feet in the ice cold stirrups and arranged my legs wide apart. The nurse adjusted my sheet to cover my knees, picked up her clip board, and stood with pen poised.

"So, what's happening, Andrews?"

"I've been bleeding almost nonstop for six months since you gave me that progesterone shot for birth control."

"It's not the shot," he said, giving me no other explanation.

"Ouch," I said, as he poked around inside me. "Do you have to do that?"

"Hand me another swab," he said, ignoring my question, talking past me to Miss Velcro who was adjusting her smock with a scritch, scritch of her fasteners.

"You know, Lynn, your vagina is atrophying," he said matter of factly. "Have you felt any discomfort in intercourse?" he asked as he put an ice cold shiny metal speculum into me and screwed it open.

"My vagina—is what?" I gasped, horrified at the shriveling vision in my head.

"Oh, your vagina doesn't look any different. The skin just begins to lose its density."

"And what does that mean?"

"God, Andrews, do you have to ask all these questions on such a busy day?"

"So far I've only asked two questions, doctor. This body is rather important to me," I said, rising up on my elbows.

Dr. Thoms's beaming face popped up over the sheet so he could see me as he patted my knee. "Andrews, you're so uptight. Relax."

"I am uptight. I've been bleeding on and off for six months."

"No, the bleeding's not good," he said, removing the speculum. "I'll give you some iron tablets and we won't use that kind of birth control again. Maybe we should do a D and C to make sure you don't have cancer."

"Iron pills and a D and C or cancer? Is that all you have to suggest?" I sat up on the table with real concern.

"Look, Andrews, I'm really busy today. We can do a blood panel if you'll make another appointment."

"I'm leaving tonight for Canada," I said.

"Take it up with my nurse."

Dr. Thoms started for the door. I reached out and grabbed his arm.

"Dr. Thoms, I've been a client of yours for twenty years. Isn't that worth another fleeting moment?"

"What is happening to women today? I'm the doctor, you know."

Just then a disembodied voice blared through the room over the intercom. "Your racketball partner says she'll meet you at the club in twenty minutes."

Dr. Thoms punched the button and said, "Thank you." He turned around, looking like a little boy with a sheepish grin.

"Dr. Thoms, sit down for a moment. I have something to tell you."

He sat on the edge of the chair that was laden with my underwear.

"I'll tell you what's going on with me, doctor. I would have told you before if you had asked. But since you didn't, I will tell you now. I'm at least premenopausal, and my hormones are out of whack. I need a blood test today, and I want to get to the bottom of this, now. When I made this appointment, I asked for a full examination, including my breasts. You're a good physician, Dr. Thoms, when you function, but you're not functioning, and that makes me furious."

Dr. Thoms stared at me awhile. "I'm sorry, Andrews. I've been an ass." He walked to the intercom. "Barbara, cancel my racket-ball appointment, and send Nancy in, please, for a blood panel. Thank you. Now, Andrews, assume the position."

I lay back down, put my feet in the stirrups, and breathed a sigh of relief. At least I had my old doctor back. He examined my breasts and gently reinserted the speculum and did a thorough exam.

"We won't know for sure until we get the blood panel back, but its a safe bet you are in menopause. Okay," he said, taking the hypodermic from Nancy and wrapping the surgical tubing around my arm. He tapped my vein over and over. I hated this. I turned my face away and then back as he plunged the needle into my skin and blood spurted all over.

"Good grief," I said as he took the needle out and stuck me a second time with a mumbled apology. When he was through making a large egg-shaped black-and-blue welt on my arm, he sat back down as Nancy left the room.

"If you take estrogen, I would suggest the patch and the lowest dosage. Do you have hot flashes?"

"Yes, thank you for asking. They are extreme."

"You should know that estrogen exposes you to breast and uterine cancer."

"How exposed?" I asked.

"No one knows. But every woman goes through this, so don't worry."

"Every woman should make me not worry?"

"You can chase estrogen with provera, progesterone pills, for five to ten days once a month, and probably you won't get uter-ine cancer. Breast—I don't know. There has not been conclusive research."

"No research—you must be kidding."

"Nope. If this were serious there surely would have been more research."

"Cancer risk and life aren't serious? If your testicles were put at risk, I don't think you would say that!"

"Well—maybe, but nevertheless, progesterone will make you cycle and slough off the endometrium and virtually erase the uterine cancer problem."

"What about women with fibroids?"

"Estrogen and provera could make them grow, but not for sure."

"Why not for sure?"

"We don't know."

"Thank you. That makes us all feel so much better," I said sarcastically.

"Well, at least the hot flashes can be controlled."

"Another Band-Aid without going to the cause."

"Perhaps, but every woman goes through this."

"So what else do I have to look forward to with my sisters?"

"Well, without estrogen, the lining of your bladder and vagina could go from forty layers of skin to four. That leaves you more open for infection and pain."

"Oh, great. What else?"

"With estrogen," he said, shifting uncomfortably, "your chance of heart disease and osteoporosis goes down almost fifty percent."

I stared at Dr. Thoms for a long time. "My bones could turn to powder, I have a fifty percent greater risk of heart disease, to say nothing of cancer, leached calcium, and painful intercourse, and you were going to leave me with no information and play racketball? Now, tell me more about osteoporosis. I understand that many women lose fifty percent of their total bone density within the first years of menopause and premenopause. And, P.S., I have trouble sleeping. What shall I do about that?"

"Take calcium and magnesium before you sleep at night. But

you do not have osteoporosis in your family. You are not too thin, you are very active, and you don't smoke. But you should take calcium anyway. You absorb calcium when you sleep, and estrogen will also help you sleep better."

"Thank you," I said. "Is there anything else I should know?"

"Not for now. Let's wait until the panel comes back." He patted my knee. "And thank you, Andrews, for being persistent. Again, I'm sorry. I do value our relationship."

"Apology accepted." Yes, I thought, if I can arrange all of this information into a healthy reality, we may still have a relationship of some kind.

BUILDING THE FIRE

―――――――――――――

ASK FOR POWER

AS YOUR BODY CHANGES

―――――――――――――

Woman at the Edge of Two Worlds reached out and touched my cheek.

"Whether you know it or not, your life has been a path down which you have searched for truth. You have made a bid for power, and you are holding your blood now. You are holding your power now. You are wise-blood now, a woman of fire. Welcome the fire when it comes, for I am the fire within."

5

THE MIRROR OF MENOPAUSE

worked with my apprentices all the next day and into the night. At midnight I fell into bed and instantly into a deep sleep. I awoke early the next morning. A shaft of sunlight, house-light as Agnes always called it, filled my bedroom. I reached out and touched the perimeter of the pool of light on my white quilt. Agnes always loved house-light. It was like a dear and beloved pet to her, and she would stroke the bars of light that came through her kitchen window. It was as if in the process of communing with that radiance she would move into her own silent, serene inner space, and for a moment the outside world would be forgotten.

I, on the other hand, leapt out of bed, swept into the bathroom that was also filled with morning sun filtering through the peach tree leaves outside the window, splashed water on my face, and ran a brush through my hair. I looked into my own eyes and heaved a deep sigh. I loved my house in Los Angeles. I had been living in this house for almost thirty years. I thought to myself, How can I even be thirty years older. Extraordinary. I ran my fingers over the tile around the sink and remembered choosing that tile with a friend of mine. It seemed like only yesterday. I looked back in the mirror again, and this time I saw the face of my

mother superimposed over mine. I smiled at her reflection, missing her so. The thought of her still made me cry. With the
thoughts of grief, I felt my skin begin to burn. My stomach and
my back filled with heat. I felt almost as if I were going to faint,
the hot flash was so intense. I made sure that I had put on my
patch, my hormone replacement therapy. I washed my face again
and, throwing a robe on, I went into the kitchen. Again, sunlight
filled the room. I took a deep grateful breath, so happy for a
sunny day. I had been raised in the Northwest, in Seattle, and I
had had enough cloudy days to last the rest of my life. There was
something about that flat light that offended my artistic eye. In
flat light there is no depth. There is just grayness. I don't enjoy
that, although some people feel it provides a cozy atmosphere
and they wrap that grayness around them like a familiar blanket.
I am not one of those people.

I made myself some Earl Grey tea and squeezed a little lemon
juice into the cup. The lemons from my tree this year were full,
round, and healthy. My little white pup, Sasha, jumped up, paw-
ing me with his front feet, wanting breakfast, wanting a biscuit,
wanting attention. I put my cup on the counter, reached down,
and picked him up and held him, scratching his ears and his
back, giving him a big good-morning kiss. I took my teacup and
walked outside to the back patio. I sat beneath the lemon tree,
smelling the fragrance of the lemon blossoms and the honeysuckle growing on the hill. Dew was still on the leaves of the
plants. It was cool in my backyard. The sun filtered through the
fuchsia-colored bougainvillea that grew in layers of scrambled
branches and flowers over the doorway leading into the kitchen.
Sasha ran back and forth, barking at imaginary coyotes on the
hill, playing with the butterflies, and finally, he came to me and
lay down on my bare feet to snooze for a moment.

I heard the phone in the other room, but I let it ring, wanting a
few more minutes of peace so I could center myself for the day.
There was a vague feeling of anxiety in my stomach. I took a
deep breath and another sip of tea, letting the steam from the liq-

uid warm my face. I closed my eyes, and breathing deeply, I moved my consciousness down into my stomach and asked myself, "Who is there inside me filling me with this strange sense of fear?" Sure enough, I found an aspect of myself—that little girl within my own being that huddles in the corner, at times crying in terror. She's afraid she will not be cared for, that she will be abandoned. It was this part of my life that carried over into adolescence and that was giving me so much difficulty during menopause. The feelings became mixed with grief and despair and caused what I thought was more difficulty with mood swings and hot flashes. I had worked with Agnes about this abandoned girl inside. When I discovered her and actively comforted her everyday in my life, my hot flashes had lessened and my anxiety went away. I even went so far as to make a small pillow that was hers, filled with scented herbs that she enjoyed. I would hold it against my stomach or in my arms as if it were a small child, and I would talk to her and give her attention. Agnes suggested I do this, as she had done, and it helped tremendously.

I moved deeply into that little girl feeling, and an image of my childhood came to me. I saw a time long ago when I was about seven years old and living on the small ranch with my father in eastern Washington state. I remembered getting up early on a cold spring morning, and we had breakfast. My father could be very loving and very supportive and sweet. We went outside and saddled my pony, Sugar, a little pinto mare who took me everywhere in those days. Dad made me a lunch, a peanut butter and jelly sandwich. I tied the lunch on the back of my saddle. I remembered getting on my horse, feeling so good, feeling my jeans against my skin, my jacket close up around my neck and shoulders.

My father and mother had separated a few months before, and she had gone on to Seattle to find work. Soon she would send for me. In the meantime I stayed with my dad. The meantime turned into a couple of years. I missed my mother terribly. I must have felt abandoned in those days. Although I understood what had happened, I knew that my father had caused the separation. I still felt so in need of my mother's love and her company. I trusted my mother. She was even tempered. My father, on the other hand, was a complex man and made life difficult for me. He would explode in fits of temper and violence. His Norwegian heritage was depressive at times, although at other times he could be warm and loving. He was the one who gave me the courage to follow my own path in life. He was the one who told me about women of power, like Babe Zaharias, the great female athlete. He would talk about her, show me black-and-white pictures of her, and take me to watch her play golf. He would talk about Esther Williams and her strength and ability in swimming. He would always tell me about women of power, and he did me a great service, because without that encouragement I don't know if I would have had the courage to search out Agnes Whistling Elk and Ruby Plenty Chiefs in those first days. It took so much courage to leave the life I knew and move into the unknown.

I thought of myself getting on my pinto mare and riding off to school. I would go to the fork in the dirt road down the street and wait for Beverly, my Native American girlfriend. She would have come up from down the road earlier, because she lived farther away. We would meet and ride off together to school, which was perhaps half a mile away. We would tether our horses out in the field where they could munch on grass. Then we would take their saddles off and go into school together. We were friends for years. It was through her and her family that I first felt my destiny would be to work with my Native American teachers. We rode together through the mountains at a very young age. We had tremendous freedom. When I look back at those days, I wonder how we survived it all without getting hurt. We would ride sometimes in one direction all day and never run into a road or another person. Many times we came across rattlesnakes, deer, and elk, a couple of times even bears, with our horses freaking out. Somehow we managed to stay on and ride home in perfect safety.

On one such morning with Beverly, riding off to school, I looked over at her, and I saw her aura, her aura of red. It was very unusual for her; she usually had green lights around her and gold. It was the first time that I ever mentioned it to her.

"The color around you is so red and orange this morning," I said. "What is wrong, Beverly?"

She flashed her dark brown eyes at me. She was very angry at her father. She told me how he had beaten her that morning. Then she said, "What do you mean red colors around me?" She told me she didn't have the faintest idea what I was talking about.

It was the first time that I realized that people didn't see colors around me as well. For some reason I had never spoken of it. I just assumed that it was a fact of life and that we all shared that experience. I remember the jolt that I felt. Suddenly I was not only the child of a divorce, which was something that was unusual in those days, but I was also a lonely child. Now I realized that I was different, and it filled me with a kind of fear. I felt lesser and like I had to cover up who I really was to fit in, to survive. I remembered fighting back the tears. Because Beverly was so immersed in her own problems and shame, she never spoke to me about it again. We remained friends all those years, but now something had come between us, between me and all people, or so I thought.

I shook my head and the remembrances away as I ran my fingers through my hair. As I sat there in my garden, a beautiful blue jay hopped down onto the table to pick up some crumbs from a cookie that I had eaten last night. I looked at that brazen bird, so grateful for its existence, and it brought me back into the present. I took a deep breath and in my mind's eye, I hugged that little girl huddling in my stomach. I held her close, folded my arms across my belly, and rocked her, telling her that everything was going to be all right, that I would take care of her. Then I laughed as Sasha looked up at me with his head cocked sideways. I thought, Yes, I probably sound like a madwoman, talking to myself. Then I said out loud to my puppy, "It's funny, isn't it, Sasha. I have had this desire to heal and to work with people all of my life, but for so long I was afraid to use my ability."

I picked up Sasha and held him close to me and let him fall asleep on my lap. I petted him as I thought about people's anxiety and how much fear there is in the world and how it's created by disowning aspects of ourselves, particularly the intuitional and instinctual aspects of our nature. When we do that we create a kind of monster that lives inside us. We create what is often termed the dark side, that part of us that is unexpressed in the world and oftentimes remains unknown even to ourselves. That child inside me is frightened because she's afraid that nobody will take care of her. To me one purpose of shamanism today is that ceremony enables you to move into those aspects of yourself that are hidden and denied and disowned. You help yourself to grow differently. You mirror those aspects of yourself, you recognize them, and you give them a voice. You allow them to express themselves in all their terror and anger so that you can then heal them. That's what it means to be a wounded healer. You go into those aspects of yourself, the wound of yourself, and you create a new environment for that energy being within you to grow and to heal.

I thought how strange it is that when a person has abilities to heal that person is often persecuted: She has been burned at the stake, crucified, or outcast. It is estimated that nine million women were burned during the Inquisition years. What a tragedy, I thought, that many people find it so hard to explore the power and abilities of inner space though we explore the boundaries of outer space. We are magnificent beings capable of extraordinary power. We have moved into the world with that power through our technology, through computers. But using that technology in the way we have, without a sense of its sacredness, is like giving a child, a baby, a sharp sword: If there is not a balance with that technological ability, a balance with meditation, with prayer, with an understanding of our sacred path in life, that child will hurt himself or someone else, just as we as human beings, armed with such power, hurt ourselves and other people. We hurt our grandchildren, all the ones who come after us.

I realized that my problems in menopause had to do with those early years when I was living with my father, who was trying so hard to be both mom and dad, my father who was struggling with his own conflicts and difficulties. Unfortunately he took much of his frustration out on me. He didn't mean to; he was doing the best he could, but it has left many scars inside me. Many aspects of myself, even with all the work that I have done, have still not been dealt with. So in menopause, I see a mirror, as I have told the women that I work with, a mirror that is unmistakable and unavoidable, that you cannot deny looking into. Now I have to own what I have become, and in these days of initiation, I realize what it is to be a changing woman. I stand at the gateway now with the great goddess, Woman at the Edge of Two Worlds, and she, indeed, is a difficult taskmaster, because there is nothing I can do to change my position. I have to learn and grow to her vision. It's like writing a book. If that book is one of wisdom, you then grow to the book—you then become the person that achievement creates and demands.

Suddenly Sasha leapt off my lap, seeing a little lizard at the end of the patio. The lizard scurried up the lattice work out of reach, and, sitting in the sun, did tiny push-ups while Sasha barked and tried to encourage the little fellow to come back down and play. I took another long sip of tea, smelling the west wind as it came down off the hill, bringing the scent of honeysuckle and pine. It was so quiet here at my home. I live up a canyon where only a few houses exist on a cul-de-sac. It was the most quiet place I could find in all of Los Angeles, a place where you cannot hear the freeways. My house lies nestled in a wild tangle of oak and lemon trees. The sumac and undergrowth cover the hills and form a carpet of green all around me. It is as if I live in the middle of the wilderness in silence.

As I looked up on the hill, I saw a doe with her young fawn nibbling on my ice plant. I was grateful that I had something that they enjoyed. Fortunately Sasha did not see them; he was too busy trying to figure out a way to climb to the lizard.

Finally, I felt better. I was fully conscious now. I set my teacup down and did my shaman dance of power in the sunlight, hearing in my mind a drumbeat, the drumbeat of Agnes Whistling Elk's sacred drum. I danced for half an hour, touching and sensing the invisible energy vectors with the tips of my fingers, smoothing the rough edges of energy. I do not know how one understands or knows the presence of such things. The sensing of the energy lines is just something that comes to you, part of what my teachers call the lodge of the body-mind. You begin to understand and feel and know the energy flows that move around the earth and back out into the universe. Our bodies are an antenna for that energy. I had known that as a child. I could feel it always and remember feeling it as a tiny baby. I wonder what gives one person the ability to see while other people have to learn to open themselves to the ability. Perhaps it is the many lifetimes that we live. Who knows. Perhaps "how" doesn't matter. The important thing is that other women and men out there, I know, have had similar experiences and have been afraid to talk about them.

After I wrote my first book, I was amazed to hear from people who have had the same experiences that I had had and had always been afraid to speak of them. They felt that they would be thought of as weird. But with the crisis that we are facing in our social and physical environment, people are perhaps finally becoming aware that we need to change the way we live, that we need to look at nature differently, not as something to consume, but as a living body to nurture. Animals are not beasts, but are magnificent beings in their own right. Everything is alive with the reflection of the Great Spirit. We are not separate. We are, in fact, all one.

I finished my dance, picked up my teacup, and went back into the house with Sasha following me. I knew that I had a half an hour before my apprentice, Linda, would arrive for her appointment. I rushed into the bathroom and turned on the shower. The phone rang. It was my secretary calling to tell me that she would be half an hour late.

6

LINDA

How can I be worried about my menopause," Linda said, "when our people have just burned the city of Los Angeles? How can I be worried about my hot flashes when all of Central L.A. was just in flames? I have lived there all of my life," Linda said, tears running down her cheeks. "I am proud to be an African-American woman," she said. She curled her long slim legs underneath her body as she sat on my couch. "I don't know how to deal with the terror that I'm feeling and the confusion, political and racial, that is chaotic and bursting out all around me. But I do know one thing, I am feeling things even more than I ordinarily feel them. I feel like my body is reacting violently to my shift in hormones. I haven't wanted to admit it to myself or anyone. If I mention hot flashes, you'd think I've said I have leprosy—not a popular subject!"

I sat on the couch next to Linda and put my arms around her. I could feel her grief and her anger, which was born from confusion more than anything else. "Linda, when I first went into menopause, I was in total denial. My mother was lying in a coma in the hospital. I would never speak to her again, and I knew it. She would never speak to me. She was incredibly important to me in my life, and I felt such loss. What was menopause in comparison to death, and yet everything is relative.

"Our inner city is being burned, but I have *always* felt such a sadness and a terror for the condition of ignorance and hatred that runs rampant through the streets of our cities. In the late seventies I worked for various trials. I volunteered for Operation Bootstrap downtown many years ago and for many other groups. Now I have dedicated my life to a different path, a path of heart instead of a path of anger. Years ago, when I saw the inequities in the world, I became deeply immersed in those inequities—the unratified treaties, the hatred, the anger, the imbalance of male and female energies in the world. And I filled my own self with hatred for my ancestors, for what my people had stood for, for political insanities that were happening everywhere. I tried to do something about that, and one day when I was marching on City Hall, something changed inside me. I felt we were getting attention momentarily, but the conditions for people were not changing, they were maybe even getting worse. 'You're trying to change the world and you need to change your life instead,' or 'got to be good looking 'cause you're so hard to see.' These lines from John Lennon touched me deeply. I understand the primal anger that people feel when they are not heard, when they wait patiently for a judgment in a case, and when the jury is in, the verdict is given that is perhaps not responsive to justice or the needs of the people. I understand, at least somewhat, what you are feeling today, Linda. But I realize in my own life that you cannot carry someone else's pain."

"I know that a man cannot carry a woman's pain, and you cannot carry the pain of another race that is not your own," Linda said.

"In realizing that, in realizing that I was, inappropriately perhaps, fighting a fight that was not mine, I changed. I discovered also that I could not sit back and watch what was happening in the world and do nothing. I wanted to find a base for communication instead of fighting without solving the original problems.

We are not separate; we are all fighting the battle for a finer and more profound life."

I watched Linda's face moving from one emotion to another, much like clouds cast fleeting shadows over the desert. "I could not live without making at least an attempt to right some of the wrongs, so I asked for a spiritual teacher, like you asked for Agnes Whistling Elk and Ruby Plenty Chiefs, and you came to me," Linda said. "I realized that out of hate, you cannot produce a more healthy society. You cannot create out of rage; you can only tear down and destroy. As I look out at this nation, I see that that is what we are so often doing, particularly in the media. We're tearing down our heroes and many ideas and people who are good and everything that is bad along with them so that nothing is left, and certainly no alternatives," Linda said defiantly.

"If someone becomes well-known for doing something, for peace, for accomplishing something that is special or unique in some way, we seem to find a reason to tear them to pieces, don't we?"

"Yes," Linda agreed. "We are left with no archetypes for our children, no heroes, no heroines, and certainly no plan for a better life. We seem to endlessly talk about what we hate. I want to understand the mysterious dimensions of healing and power. I want to go to the source of the disease that lives within us all and find a way to heal it. When I looked at our world, so bereft of balance, I had to find what is missing, like you did."

"I believe that female consciousness is the piece of the puzzle that has been lost. My journey with the Sisterhood is about empowering women, empowering myself, and nurturing a life-giving approach to all living things." I paused for a moment and looked carefully at Linda's aura, which had moved from predominantly red and filled with anger and frustration to more green that indicated to me that her heart was opening. "In a sense, Linda, menopause comes along at a very interesting time in life, and in your case, in history. Don't you think?"

"Yes, I do."

"It is a time when perhaps half of your life has been lived, and yet, half of your life is yet to be lived. Because of that kind of halfway point, it is almost as if the Great Spirit planned this to coordinate with your political life and said, 'This is a time for you to take stock, Linda. Take stock of where you stand with the people. Take stock of how you are living, of what you have created.' You have created so much in your world. You have become an enormously successful woman. You have managed to be within the political system, and yet not become a victim of it. You still live in the neighborhood where you were brought up. Your social life has not changed. You're not beholden to political interests that could have bought you off long ago."

I could see that Linda was beginning to brighten. She sipped her tea. "I am doing my work and speaking out from my heart without fear, and if people get angry with my point of view, so be it. It is an honest point of view, and I really honor myself for that. Not to change the subject, but when I'm publicly speaking, I'm mixing up my words or I find myself losing words. Is that because of menopause, too?"

"Yes," I laughed, "sometimes I feel like my mind has gone south for the season. Agnes suggested I might try a homeopathic remedy called Kali carb, and it really worked for me. You can find it in health food stores."

"Wow! I'd really like to get over that," Linda said. We laughed together in deep understanding.

"Menopause is an opportunity, perhaps, Linda, for you to acknowledge with your sisters that here is a time for sisterhood within the bleakness of seeming political and sociological desolation. Perhaps now it is time for a true sisterhood to form within your people, a sisterhood out of love and not out of hatred, a sisterhood out of building creativity that can create a new world, that can create new ideals, that can create new education and a new format for life. You have, because of the situation that you have grown out of, a tremendous bonding with the people that you live with. Adversity often brings us closer in a special kind of way."

Linda nodded and dried her tears. She looked into my eyes for a long time. "I am finding what you say and our spiritual work together to be so empowering. Most of my fears have dissipated," she said. "I am taking sacred time for myself. I am meeting with my sisters and healing old wounds with my family. My therapist is also helping me with my relationships. She also honors deeply our process of shamanism, as you honor her work. Many of my sisters are acknowledging a bond of experience during the change. I went to my gynecologist as you suggested, Lynn, and I was given a prescription for the estrogen patch and provera. I am wearing it. It seems to be very good for me. I feel much stronger. Homeopathic remedies worked for my mother but not for me. What was happening to me, Lynn, is I was getting physically weak, and I have found that since I have been on the patch and with provera, I have been feeling stronger. I feel like there is a new balance, somehow, in my body. I wish that I could bring that same kind of balance back to my people. I feel so frightened for what has happened in Los Angeles during these days, because I feel that all the strides that we have made for racial equality, for building a better society for the black people has been set back years and years. I feel like my heart is broken."

"You've been having heart palpitations at night, haven't you?" I asked after a long pause.

Linda looked at me wide-eyed. "Did I mention that?"

"No," I said.

"Well, then how—"

"Look at what you just said."

"What?"

"'My heart is broken,' but it's not just because of the riots."

Linda stared at me and then a cloud of sadness enveloped her. "Oh, God," she said. "It's true, isn't it, because of menopause and everything that's happening in my life. I'm brokenhearted.

Could that really cause me to have heart trouble or at least heart stress?"

"What do you think?" I asked.

"Will you help me? Those palpitations scare me."

"Linda, I can't help you. You can only help yourself. But I am trained to See you. I will hold up mirrors for you. If you have the courage, you will see what you need to change. Spend the next few weeks witnessing yourself and your heart. Between you and me, I know you'll heal yourself. You just had to see it. That's your secret. The estrogen will help as well."

We sat quietly for awhile, and then Linda said, "I will witness myself. So what next?"

"One thing I want to mention to you. In Chinese medicine, they talk about kidney yin and yang deficiency during menopause. You have spoken about hot flashes, sweating palms, a lowered sex drive, and extreme tiredness, which are symptoms to the Chinese of different energy needs that can be treated by acupuncture and herbs. I would strongly suggest that you look into this. If you can get off chemical replacements and still be healthy and comfortable, it would probably be wise. Don't you agree?"

"Okay, I'll really look into it, Lynn."

"Well, perhaps, Linda, just as you went for help for your body, just as you went for help for your own spirituality and sacredness, perhaps you can find an archetype within the blue print of your own body and health that relates to your own society."

Linda looked at the palms of her hands and then she picked up a jasper sphere sitting on the table in front of her and held it up to the light. It was various shades of brown, and there was a cohesiveness and a beauty to the sphere in how it reflected the light.

"You know, this sphere is like people, in a way, isn't it?" Linda said. "It is varicolored and yet each hue, one color laid upon another, makes it very beautiful, like a sacred dance. We are in a sacred dance of nationalities in a way, and I know that, Lynn. I know what you teach—that to be caught in this crazy dream that we are living without a spiritual perspective is to lose in the long run. I know that on some level this is all an illusion. As you taught me so well, I know the depth of seriousness in this life that leads toward enlightenment. And I know that it's all a teaching. I know that all of this trauma and pain and anger and difficulty is also a teaching that is going to force all of us to change, hopefully for the good, and I see that. I see that in my own body as well. I see that I'm being forced to look at the woman that I am, and I see certain things that I don't like."

"What is that, Linda? What is it that you could possibly not like about yourself?" I had tremendous admiration for this woman who had stood up against her own leaders many times and had educated people through their veils of misunderstanding into a place of communication. I held respect for her. She was very beautiful.

"I find, Lynn," she said, still holding the sphere and enjoying its coolness against her cheek, "that menopause is a great opportunity to take some time off, just as you say." She giggled. "Time off from the stress of my political life and come back to me, because in the end as you have often told me, 'Don't forget who you are. You are of the goddess, of the Great Spirit, of whoever your god is.' I am not a woman politician; I am a woman living my truth who happens to work in politics and community government. For a long time I had forgotten that. I lost my balance, but interestingly, in preparing for our ceremony with Woman at the Edge of Two Worlds, I see myself more clearly, and I am changing in every way."

I nodded in agreement with her. "Yes, that really is what menopause is about. That's why it's so important to change the way we view menopause, because I think that no matter how humorously we speak of menopause and hot flashes, no matter how much we laugh at the circumstances we find ourselves in, this is a very serious passage. It does have to do in a profound way with the rest of your life, and there are none of us who love getting older. Perhaps we love the wisdom and the knowledge that we have gained and the experiences that we have had, but we do not particularly enjoy watching our bodies slowly move closer and closer to the earth. There is no question that this is a time to take stock of the past, but most important, I believe," I said, "it is important to look forward into the future, because we do not want to repeat in the future the inequities of the past. All of society is learning that. It's almost as if all of us—governments, social orders, countries, educational systems, religious organizations, and a great population of women—are going through a men-o-pause in a way."

"I'll drink to that," Linda said, sipping her lemon tea and lying back against the couch with a heavy sigh.

"We are reclaiming our spirit," I urged. "Is that not true?"

"Well, then, I feel in a sense I have lost my spirit. Sometimes I get so terribly tired, I don't know how I can continue to live."

I nodded agreement, for surely I had felt that way often myself. I watched Linda's lights as they began to merge into green shaded with pink and golden white. She was integrating her mind with her physical being.

"But we have each other, Linda; we have each other and a sisterhood that is so profound. Perhaps the finest lesson of the menopause, the change of life, is that we do change our life, and we reach out our hands, not only across racial and cultural boundaries, but to our sisters, and we join in a circle of experience that we all have. No matter where we came from, no matter where we're going, this is one experience that we all have in common, so let's celebrate this experience. Yes, we are losing something, and I know that you feel that deeply, because I know that you wanted to have another child."

"Yes, I really did," Linda said. "My husband and I have tried for years and years to have another child, but I guess it just wasn't in the cards."

"But you already have a beautiful daughter, Linda."

"I know, but my husband so much wanted to have a son."

"Well, maybe next time," I said, smiling.

"Yes, maybe next time. But you see," Linda continued, "as much as I am concerned with my life in the government, I'm also concerned about my husband, because when he realized I was going through menopause, and I must admit I hid it from him for a long time, I saw the disappointment and the pain in his face. It's like a thing that he can't get over, like he's blaming me for cheating him in some way, that somehow he will never have a son and that's all because of me, that it's all my fault."

"But Linda, it's not your fault. It's just the circumstance, as you well know."

"Yes, I know, Lynn, but that doesn't stop my emotions from going wild in the middle of the night when I wake up unable to sleep and my husband has turned away from me."

"Linda, I think perhaps you should bring Larry with you, and we should talk about this."

"Oh, no, Lynn, he would never come. He would never come. He cannot speak of personal things in front of other people. It's a very private affair to him. In fact, he won't even speak about it to me."

"Well, perhaps, when we have our celebration, when we have our initiation, when you meet on a ceremonial level Woman at the Edge of Two Worlds, perhaps in the celebration afterward Larry can come and take part in that ceremony."

"But how could that be possible? This is only for women."

"No," I said, "it's for your whole family. It's not just for you."

"Really?" she said.

"Yes, and I want that to be, because just as a young girl going into puberty should be celebrated by her whole family, so should you be celebrated by your whole family. After all, you are now becoming the elder, the wise one, the respected one, and that does not mean the ugly one, the old wrinkled crone, but the wise, beautiful crone. Yes, perhaps we are headed for wrinkles as well, but that doesn't mean that you've lost the substance of your beauty. You are a magnificently attractive woman. Whatever your age may be, you are moving into a very sacred time, and that should be shared by all and revered by all. And it will be. I think I can promise you that. I know Larry is a thoughtful man. He will understand, because after all, he's going through his own kind of energy shifts, his own kind of menopause."

Linda's eyebrows lifted, as she looked at me questioningly.

"Oh, yes, Linda, men go through menopause, too, of a different kind. They do not necessarily lose their fertility, but they do shift and change, and even on a physical level their testosterone levels shift. Haven't you seen some elderly women whose voices drop and they become overly pugnacious and strong? That's because their testosterone levels rise in relationship to the estrogen levels that drop. Also, their yang energy often rises and the yin drops and needs to be balanced. They become more masculine. Lots of times men, as they get older, lose their testosterone levels and they become more feminine, more receptive, and more yin. Sometimes they even look transparent standing next to their wives. You know what I mean?"

"Yes, I do, I guess. I never thought of that," she said. "Although I must say my grandma is a pistol."

"That's what I mean."

"Hmm," she said. "She did become much more dominant as she got older."

"You know, some of our traditions in the Sisterhood of the Shields talk about the sacred clown and how the beginnings of the sacred clown came with menopause. You see evidences of such social transformations in the South, for instance, where women were so restricted in their behavior; as soon as they become menopausal they move into a different stage of life. They are then allowed, through a mutual respect by everyone in society, to become outrageous. Their stories become outrageous. They speak often in an eccentric and challenging way. Many societies are like this, and it is a kind of respect that allows women to behave without the usual restraint."

"Really?" she said.

"Yes, I have some books I will share with you. Just in terms of history this is true, and the Sisterhood speaks of it. I think Twin

Dreamers is a really wonderful example of a woman, an elder woman, who behaves almost without restraint. I don't mean without responsibility; I mean without limits in regards to what a woman is supposed to do or not supposed to do. She goes beyond the limits of even ordinary reality, because she is a shape shifter and helps you to experience her in different form—maybe very young or old, maybe as a hawk. She can move wherever she wishes. It is her power, and she has cultivated that power. It began for her during menopause."

"Is that right? Twin Dreamers was always one of my very favorite women of the Sisterhood," she said. "I loved reading about her in *Star Woman*. She was so fascinating, the way she healed with her laughter."

"Yes, it is a great art, and unfortunately, a disappearing one. But as long as Twin Dreamers and Ruby are around, they certainly won't let it disappear all together."

We both laughed. I took the sphere from Linda's hands, and I too held it up to the sunlight streaming in through the windows. There was also white there within the jasper, probably pieces of granite. It was a sphere that had been brightly shined, beautiful and perfect. It felt smooth, like soft, warm caramel in my hands.

"This sphere represents the earth to me," I said. "When I move into double dreaming, into other levels of consciousness, I use this sphere. Oftentimes I look into her and I see aspects of our physical reality reflected there. I see the beauty and the power of all races combined into a living whole of beauty and caring, something that we all need to learn and experience. Perhaps with this shift in the whole social climate around the earth and our cities, we can bring about a more deeply sensitized communication between all people sooner than we ever thought, sooner than we ever dreamed," I said as rain began to play a staccato beat on the roof.

"Oh, so be it," Linda said, bowing her head. "Thank you, sister."

7

EVEN AS YOU STAND BEWILDERED

I spent several hours doing ceremony and thinking about Linda after she left. Then I gathered my rain gear and headed for the equestrian center in Burbank where I took a riding lesson with Pam. Afterward, we were both famished. So, since Agnes had told me to go to the health food store to pick up certain vitamins and herbs, I thought we might as well go there to eat.

"Come on, Pam," I urged my less than enthusiastic friend, "health food stores have great sandwiches."

"I hate health food," Pam grumbled. "We may as well eat alfalfa out of the horses' stalls."

"You don't have to eat sprouts or tofu," I laughed. "I promise, they'll have something you'll like."

"All right. I'm so hungry I could eat almost anything." She shook her head and gave me a little half smile. "You take a lot out of me, you know."

Pam laughed good naturedly and prodded me with her elbow as we walked into the store. It was teeming with the usual mix of Los Angeles humanity. The aisles were crowded with large women in Birkenstock sandals, pushing overloaded carts with children swaying dangerously from their backpacks while they grabbed bottles from the shelves. Men and women from Asia,

Africa, Saudi Arabia, and South America clamored for assistance in a cacophony of jumbled languages. As Pam and I glanced at each other, wondering if we'd stepped onto the set of *Aliens,* an elderly couple, trying to stay out of the way, pushed a cart bearing a black scotty dog into an overstocked shelf and a barrage of brown plastic vitamin C bottles cascaded down upon the whole cowering company.

Trying to avoid the melee, we walked carefully to the yellow and green capped bottles in the herbal section. I picked up a bottle and tried to read the label with my once-perfect vision. But my efforts were in vain. All I could see was a blur of black and white.

"Pam, can you read this?"

I turned to find my friend, but she had vanished in the cheese-cloth-turbaned and rainbow-clad throng. Just as I opened my purse to find my glasses, an unidentified elbow sent me sprawling to my knees. Everything in my purse scattered across the floor.

"Oh, I'm so sorry," a male voice murmured. I turned to see a shaved-headed, orange-robed saint with a tin cup and brightly colored books extended into my face. He had slipped on a brown banana peel and was regaining his balance. "I thought I might interest you in enlightenment," he said, tapping the book with his cup.

"You could give me a hand," I said with astonishment at his gall.

"Oh, sure," he said, turning to leave. "I'll be right back."

The orange-clad saint twirled around toward the elderly couple and cornered them against a shelf full of organic cheese puffs and soybean chips. Realizing that he had no intention of helping me to my feet, I began scrambling around on my hands and knees to the accompaniment of low growls from the scotty dog. Cursing under my breath, I picked up my valuables—a tampon in case I hemorrhaged unexpectedly, a bent tube of Borofax originally manufactured for diaper rash that I always apply liberally to my dry and cracking lips, a bottle of homeopathic eye drops for any unforeseen allergy attacks, some digestive aids, my wallet, and, of course, the glasses that I was presently blaming for this entire fiasco.

"I can't leave you alone for a moment," Pam said, half laughing, half concerned, as she joined me on the floor to see what I was doing.

"Don't even ask," I said. "It's too long a story."

Laughing together, Pam and I righted ourselves, and I again began my herbal search. I took a bite of the cashew bar coated with carob that Pam thrust into my mouth as I read another label in my endless quest. About that time a small gentleman with a kind face saw me struggling through the bottles and came to my rescue.

"May I help you?" he asked.

"I thought you would never ask," I said, smiling at the friendly face. "I'm looking for black cohash."

"We don't have that isolated," he answered, "but here is a good change-of-life formula." He handed me a white bottle with a pink top. "Certainly not for you." He smiled, looking me up and down. "You're much too young."

I liked him immediately. "You're right," I said, "but it seems that my mind and my body are in disagreement on that subject."

He smiled and nodded his head sagely. "Now, dear lady, how else may I help you?"

I handed him my list, and he began ushering me up and down the aisles, helping me make the proper selections. I was just beginning to enjoy myself when Pam finally reached the limits of her patience.

"Lynn, for heaven's sake, will you hurry up? Can't you get your hot flash ointment some other time? I'm getting hungrier by the minute and there's nothing edible in this entire place."

"Our tofu and sprout sandwiches are especially good today," the little man said innocently.

Pam simply stared at my newfound friend. "Lynn, this place is noisier and crazier than a three ring circus. I'll wait for you outside."

The noise level had seemed to increase in the store. I began to wonder how health could be gleaned from such a chaotic atmosphere. In the past I had only come to this store during its off-hours and had always found a wellspring of herbs and information. So I was no more prepared for the chaos than was my uninitiated younger companion.

As my tiny savior rang up my purchases, my mind fled to a peaceful retreat within my memory where I could smell the clean scent of Canadian pine and feel a gentle rain on my face. I heard Agnes's voice singing an old ceremonial chant to the beat of her medicine drum. Swaying inside to the music of her chant, I remembered her words to me.

"We are one with Mother Earth—to heal her, we must first heal ourselves and the people who destroy her. Hear my voice singing in all the named and nameless things, and love all that lives, even as you stand bewildered on the streets in the great cities of the world."

IGNITING THE FIRE

The great goddess knelt before me. She swept her fingers across the diagrams on the floor of the cave, sending flames around my feet and up the walls.

"Your fears are like tethers on your feet. They keep you from moving toward the sky with the flames. You are like water, my apprentice. You flow downward toward the earth. I must heat you up. I will turn your body into steam, and we will rise together toward the heavens."

8

FREEWAY MAGIC

I looked out at the gray flannel sky, the imprint of clouds barely visible through the sheeting rain that surrounded me as I sped down the freeway toward home. Occasionally, trees would loom up out of the mist on either side of the road. There were four lanes of traffic in my direction, all of us traveling sixty-five-miles per hour, or seventy, through the torrents of water washing all around us, through the blasts of wind that would come and go. We were isolated from one another. The rain was so dense that we couldn't see into each other's car windows, but here we were by some strange twist of fate, coursing down the freeway in the same direction, leading to private destinations unknown. If any one of us veered out of our lane, certain death or maiming would occur. Yet we stayed in our own little lanes, trusting that we knew where we were going, trusting that every person on that freeway could handle their own car or truck and would not veer into our lane without warning. We were in the same energy flow, and yet we did not know each other. I was curious about what brought us together at this time, about fate in life. Had we ever known each other in other lifetimes? Perhaps the black jeep I was driving next to contained someone I had known intimately in another lifetime. Who knows, but we are all going in the same direction, if only for this short time.

When I moved into menopause, I felt like I was out of control. It is something that every woman goes through, but that doesn't mean that we speak of it. It is an uncharted passage, a passage into a vast unknown. Nearly half of our life will be lived after menopause. We all course down the same freeway, the same track, most of us isolated from one another like so many cars on a freeway, wondering about our destination, wondering if we will reach it safely and whole, without disaster, without disease, without some unforeseen energy force veering into our lane of life and disrupting our journey.

Up ahead a brightly lit, blinking sign said SLOW, PREPARE TO STOP, ACCIDENT AHEAD. How like that is our position in life, where suddenly because our physiology has changed, because we no longer menstruate, the chance of heart disease increases by fifty percent. If we take estrogen to delay that event, to hopefully keep that from ever happening to us, we then incur the possibility of cancer. What a strange effect that knowledge must have on our subconscious mind. It's bad enough that we live with the threat of earthquake at any moment, of nuclear war at any moment, of diseases ready to land on you if your immune system is inadequate or stressed or fatigued. Who in the world lives today without stress and fatigue? It is no wonder that when we learn about atrophying vaginas and all these uncontrollable things that are going to happen to us now, that we get frightened, that we go into ourselves and pretend that it isn't happening. We pretend that life is going along as it always has with a big smile and a joke. But inside, how can we not "take pause"? Besides everything else, we sense that there is a gateway here. We sense, perhaps, that now is a time to sit still for a moment in our own silence and truth, and begin to examine what we have created in our lives. It's a time to own what we have become. It is a time to reckon with our created lifestyle and relationships. That is the beginning of initiation. You begin to sit still, to look at the choices that you have made. Some of them have been good, some of them have not, and you grieve for those choices that were incorrect, for the tragedies of life that everyone has experienced. In the process of initiation, you give away. You give away your grief. You give away old baggage. You go on a vision quest, and you take time alone to reconsider your life path, to reconsider what it means to be woman.

In shamanism my teachers have taught me to see signs in the world, that things do not happen by accident. I am now stopped on the freeway, and I look in front of me at a license plate that says IRON TREE. I think, it is true, isn't it? Women are made of iron. We are asked to be everything. We have always been asked to endure, and so often we endure silently. We don't express the quiet desperation of our difficult marriages, the desperation and solitude of raising children at home, isolated so often from the world. We have the feeling, as Betty Friedan put so well in her book *The Feminine Mystique,* that we, as women, often feel that the world is going on without us. How do we reclaim that movement into the world? How do we feel a part of things again? Menopause is another mark where we have to maintain our strength quietly, and we feel again separated from the world and what's happening with younger people or women who haven't yet experienced this event.

In the old way, there was always a ceremony and there was always a dance and a feast. The dance of a traditionally sacred life was wonderful and gave you a sense of oneness with your creator. That unity can be found once again. We dance in initiation. We dance into initiation and out on the other side. That is what I would like to bring to you. If you do not feel separate, if you do not feel any of these aspects that I speak of in menopause—although I can't quite imagine if you are honest and truthful with yourself how you do not, but maybe you don't—maybe this is something you can just take in stride; maybe you are that strong, and that is wonderful, but nevertheless it is an event that should be marked, because it is a powerful transition.

You are moving from a woman, a reproductive woman who was capable of creating a family, into a world of wise-blood, "wise-blood" meaning that you hold your blood and your power and its wisdom. You become the elder; you become the teacher; you become the spirit woman for your people. To move into that initiation, dance is a wonderful celebration, because in dance, you sense the inspiration of spirit, and you become that inspiration through your own movement, through your own expression. You express your sacredness as you are. So I will teach you to dance in this initiation, because this initiation is about unity. It is about sisterhood; it is about celebration of your power as it relates to your god or goddess.

Suddenly the cars began to move in a steady flow like the rain. We seem to have been curtailed for no reason, as so often happens in life. There was no evidence of obstruction. I settled back in my seat and took a deep breath. As I felt a new flow of energy moving down the freeway, I felt a deepened resolve within myself, unblocked, and a freer sense of relatedness to such a seemingly alien world. Agnes had taught me to see life as a challenge and to take every moment as a gift, no matter how frustrating the situation, even if it is a traffic jam on the freeway. Fortunately, I would be back home in time for my appointment with Phyllis, a woman I had not worked with before.

9

PHYLLIS

I'm not interested in shamanism," the woman said carefully as she folded her hands neatly in her lap. We were sitting in my living room. It was a cold, blustery day, but the rain had stopped. The fire danced in the fireplace, adding an aura of warmth and comfort to our otherwise difficult meeting.

"If you're not interested in shamanism, Phyllis, then I can't help you," I said.

"What do you mean?"

"Well, I'm not a psychotherapist, so I'll have to send you to someone else. I can suggest a wonderful woman who studied at Stanford."

"But I don't want a therapist. I'm sorry, I guess what I'm really interested in is you and your experiences."

"We can talk a little about that if you like, as long as you understand that I do not practice psychotherapy in any way. I only train people in the way of shamanism that I have learned. Okay?"

"Okay."

"Would you like to talk to me a little bit, Phyllis, about your feelings having to do with shamanism? Do you understand what shamanism is about?"

"All I know is it sounds weird," Phyllis stated very emphatically as she reached for her cup of tea and took a sip, holding the cup finally in the palm of her hand. "And I'm really tired of hearing about auras and other states of consciousness and space travel, or whatever you call it."

"Astral travel," I interjected.

"Really, Lynn, I don't mean to be rude. I have read your books and I enjoyed them as adventure stories. I liked the way you took your power and learned about yourself. That's what's important to me. But shamanism sounds like something too far out for me, and . . . I really don't know why I'm here."

Phyllis started to cry, and I handed her a tissue. Her cheeks were crimson, and there were beads of perspiration on her forehead. I could see the perspiration on her scalp and on the backs of her hands. I could tell that she was having a hot flash. She took the tissue and wiped the back of her neck. Finally, heaving a sigh, she sat back into the couch and looked at me in a state of total desperation.

"I am married to a man who is very powerful," Phyllis said.

I nodded.

"He is head of a film studio and he likes his life to be uncomplicated at home, because in the office it is so complicated." She started to cry again. "For the last year and a half, even though I take progesterone and estrogen, I am out of control. I'm in menopause. My emotions have become an enemy inside me. At the strangest times I seem to fall apart, and it's causing a great rift in my marriage. My husband has taken to sleeping in another room, because all night long I am hot and cold, hot and cold, throwing off the covers, and frankly, Lynn, I'm miserable and I don't know where else to turn. I'm sorry if I've insulted you. It wasn't what I meant to do, but I can see that you have found some answers. Perhaps you can help me to find some." Again, she started to cry into her tissue.

I sat with her for a long time. After a while, I asked her gently, "Phyllis, what was your dream as a child? What did you envision your life being when you grew up?"

Phyllis's face brightened. Her brunette hair was carefully combed straight and fell just below her jaw line, with bangs over her forehead that hid the wrinkles that were there and showed occasionally when she flipped her head in a very youthful manner. She was a very attractive woman in a sophisticated way. She wore a lovely beige cashmere sweater, skirt and stockings, and simple but expensive shoes. Her entire look was tailored and well-kept. Suddenly the dampness on her face shone with the exuberance of her expression as she moved from a mood of great sadness into almost childlike excitement.

"Oh, Lynn, I always wanted to dance. I danced out of the womb, I think." She giggled to herself. "My mother was a ballerina in Russia, and she married my father and defected from Russia very early on. We lived in New York. My father was from a very well-to-do political family. Even though my mother was famous for her dancing—they called her Lillian—my father's family felt that it was inappropriate for her to dance any longer. It was not appropriate for her to be on the stage, to be an entertainer, even though she was far more than an entertainer. She was a great artist. They felt that it did not fit with the family image, and so she gave up her life as a dancer and had me and my three brothers. I always wanted to dance, and even though my mother took me to dancing classes of all kinds, she made it very clear to me that this wasn't something I would ever do professionally. Dancing was fitting for a lady only if done in private. Except for the few recitals I did as a child, I never pursued my dream."

Again, she started to cry. This time I could see that her sweater was becoming wet. She was soaking wet from head to toe.

"Come." I took her hand, which was also wet, and led her to the bathroom. I handed her a towel, soft and pink, and she buried her face in it. She wore no makeup, except for a little mascara. Her lipstick had already been rubbed off. I said, "Take your time, Phyllis. I'll be waiting in the living room."

Fifteen minutes later, Phyllis came back into the living room, her hair freshly combed, her face dry at last. I handed her a glass of ice water, which she gratefully downed in several swigs. She sat again across from me and this time smiled in a much more relaxed way. I put on some music.

"It's very nice," she said, her shoulders imperceptibly beginning to sway to the beat. Then I took a drum that was at my feet and I handed it to her. "Oh," she said, "I don't know how to play musical instruments."

"It doesn't matter. Just hold the drum like this." I took another drum and held it by the strings on the back. I picked up a mallet and indicated for her to do the same. She picked up the mallet. "Now, Phyllis, forget the woman you are in everyday life, just for a moment. Obviously, some of the things that you are doing are not working, so give yourself a chance to be different for a moment. You are safe here; there is no one to see. Let's play a little."

I began to beat the drum to the music, and very quickly Phyllis followed my lead, and presently, we were drumming wildly to the music that was rising to a crescendo all around us in the speakers. After a while, I stood up. She kicked off her high heels and stood up with me. We went to the center of the room.

"Phyllis, close your eyes," I said. "Close your eyes and let your knees bend like this."

I bent down and then up and down and then up with the rhythm of the music. I had her close her eyes, and as she did, a look of ecstatic relaxation crossed her face and her head began to move to the rhythm. She was very good with her body. It was clear that she had a highly tutored sense of rhythm, a strong centeredness in her physical body.

"Dream, Phyllis, let your mind drop away, and let your imagination take you into a meadow in the wilderness. The green grass is verdant and lush. There is dew on the petals of the flowers. Tiny blue bells, yellow mustard grass, and beautiful daisies, white with black centers, carpet the ground. There are birds flying over and the clouds are billowing and soft. Keep drumming; keep up the rhythm. Just imagine yourself walking through the meadow. You have on a long skirt that catches on the tops of the grass. You are wearing sandals. You feel a gentle breeze coming up from the south on your cheeks, and it blows through your hair."

We played for a long time, walking through this meadow together in our minds. At the moment I felt she was ready, when I could see that her energy field was filled with the color green and her heart had opened wide so that she was vulnerable and moving into an almost childlike sweetness and grace, I suggested that she begin to dance.

"Phyllis, move with the rhythms that we are creating. Move with the sound of the music, not any specific steps, but just move. If you wish to put the drum down, do so. I will continue to play. Let yourself enjoy the feeling that you are having at this moment. I know that you are feeling expanded and warm and that you are in a state of a kind of bliss. Just let yourself go with it. Enjoy it. Have some fun."

Phyllis bent low from the waist, and placed her drum carefully on the floor, and hiking her skirt above her knees, she held out her arms like an eagle in flight and she began to swoop and sway with the music. She leapt into the air suddenly, and from the depth of her spirit, she let out a call that for all the world sounded like a bird of prey. She swished around my living room, dipping and twirling and leaping. She was laughing joyously. Then she began to sway very quietly in front of the window. The light coming through the lemon tree was playing off the shine of her hair, accentuating the graceful and alive quality of her body and the contours of her beautiful skin. She relished in the feeling of the sun warming her body. She relished her feelings of freedom.

"Dance is very sacred," I said. "It is more than just movement. When an artist creates a painting, she thinks about her painting. She intuits that painting. But then she has to go outside herself to create that work of art, and that creates a duality. What has happened in your life is that you have created a duality. There is you and then there is a whole other world out there. You have not felt a part of that world for a long time. When a poet creates her writing, she must write it on a piece of paper, and it exists separate from her even though she created it. In the creation of a piece of art is a kind of bliss that comes from the Great Spirit, from your god, whoever that may be. It is a feeling of inspiration and joy. It is the true art of inspiration that makes us happy. It is the state of oneness with all life that we are all searching for.

"Phyllis, you have that ability. You have known of this ability since you were very young, but you have disowned this ability, because you were taught that it was incorrect. Perhaps now you can reclaim that part of yourself that you have given away. Perhaps you can reclaim what is yours, what you have always known to be true. No wonder you have been sad and desperate. No wonder your menopause is difficult. You have given away parts of yourself that you are now coming face-to-face with. They are mirrors for your enlightenment. I know these words are difficult for you, but for a moment, keep dancing. Keep feeling that ecstatic quality inside you."

I left her alone now. I sat and I drummed. The music played over and over again, and finally, after at least an hour had gone by, Phyllis collapsed on the floor, lying on her back, gasping for air, laughing uproariously. I got her another glass of ice water, and finally she sat up.

"Phyllis, that was beautiful. You have danced magnificently. How do you feel?"

After drinking the entire glass of water, she reached out to me with both hands and gave me a big hug. Tears rolled down her cheeks, but this time they were tears of happiness. "I don't know what to say," she said, "except thank you. I thought that I would sit here today and come back hour after hour, year after year, and we would talk. I never dreamed that"—she looked at her watch—"in two hours' time that my life could be changed. I can't begin to tell you how different I feel."

"It's not a miracle, you know. You did it."

"What were you saying before about artists and duality?"

"I was saying that the dance becomes the dancer, the dancer becomes the dance. When you dance, you become the living expression of your art. There is a oneness that is created with your source of inspiration. That source is life force, the Great Spirit that animates you."

Phyllis stared at me. Then searching through her purse, she found a small spiral notebook and pen and began taking notes. Her brunette hair fell forward over her eyes. She tossed her head and kept on writing. I watched a large gray squirrel jump from the mulberry tree onto the railing of the balcony. She switched her tail and chattered at her own reflection in the window.

"A good sign," I said, indicating the squirrel outside.

"What?" she asked.

"A squirrel is a sign of family. She gathers nuts and seeds of knowledge for later use."

"You have done so much for me, out of nowhere, out of nothing," she said.

"No, Phyllis, I haven't done anything for you except love you and see you. I have been taught how to *see* the energy in people. I have been taught how to heal, how to hold up mirrors for you, and if you have the courage to look in those mirrors—and that's the trick—you can change your life. I can provide an environment for you to grow, but it is your choice to grow."

"You mean you can take a horse to water but you can't make him drink?" she laughed.

"That's right. You choose to reclaim those aspects of yourself that have been denied, don't you?"

Phyllis took a deep breath and looked outside at the sun shining through the fuchsia bougainvillea. She twisted her head this way and that. Her neck was obviously stiff.

"It's important for you to be right, isn't it, Phyllis?"

I could hear her neck cracking. She swung around and looked at me.

"Yes, I guess it is. How did you know that?"

"I can see it in your neck. Your neck is very stiff, isn't it? It's stiff in the back of your neck."

"Yes, I can hardly turn it."

"Well, you need to be right. You need to know that you are right about something, because everything seems to be wrong, and you don't want to admit it."

"Yes, you're right. Again, you're right," she said, laughing. "Oh, my god, I feel like I have so much to learn, and you have shown me that, Lynn. You have shown me that there is a whole new world out there and that there is hope."

We got up off the floor and went back to the couch. I sat in my chair to the left, nearly facing her.

"When I first met my teacher, Agnes Whistling Elk," I said, "she taught me about the sacredness of birds and all living things."

I was holding a feather and stroking it with my fingers to smooth it. It was a hawk feather that Ruby had given me years ago, and I used it often in my work with people. It gave me strength and reminded me that we are all here to reflect the Great Spirit and send messages to him when we can in the form of prayer.

"When I first sat in Agnes Whistling Elk's cabin, I looked into her face, and I saw the woman that I wanted to learn from. She had such power and simplicity about her, and she looked at me and laughed. She always laughs at me, you know, Phyllis, and I will laugh a lot at you. It is not really at you, but with you. The purpose is to move you off your seriousness and your desperate need to be right, because we are only right part of the time, and so often we are so wrong. Anyway, Agnes looked at me with that piercing look of hers, and she said, 'You and I sit on either side of a chasm. You are on one side of the Grand Canyon. Imagine that,' and she slapped her thigh and giggled at me, 'and I stand over here in peace and freedom and joy. Our work together is a process of building a bridge across this great chasm. It's a rainbow bridge of light and is built from your trust that I know what I am talking about. You have to trust me, Lynn, because otherwise we will make no headway. You stand over there on your side of the chasm with a millstone around your neck.' 'What do you mean,' I had asked her. 'That millstone is composed of your self-imposed fears and ideas. You have a fence around your consciousness. The ability to drop that millstone is accomplished with our process of teaching. What will happen is that you will chip away at that millstone slowly, year after year, until one day you will drop it and then you will have built a bridge across that chasm, and then it is faith that you will need to make the first step out into the abyss. You sit over there, Lynn, in powerlessness, and I sit over here in power. How do I move you from where you are to where I am?'

"And Phyllis, it begins as we began today. We work together, and I hold up mirrors for you, and you work as fast as you can work. It's up to you. You can be enlightened in a day, in a moment, and sometimes it takes a thousand lifetimes. But remember, there has to be trust and faith in yourself, in your own basic goodness, in your own basic power and intent to be whole."

Phyllis looked at me, her eyes round and saucerlike. "I am amazed," she said. "I am amazed by the simplicity of what has happened here today, but tell me, Lynn, what does this have to do with menopause?"

"All of this has to do with menopause, because I have a sense that in your adolescent years, you probably had a great desire to train to be a dancer. Is that not true?"

"Yes, it is. It's absolutely true."

"You were curtailed from your dream," I said.

"Yes, I had to deny myself. It was more appropriate for me to go to a good Eastern girls' school, and I studied humanities, and I felt lost and sad. I had a period of great depression in adolescence, when I was about sixteen. I had a great difficulty to the point where I had to leave school. My father and mother were mostly angry at me more than anxious. They were furious that I wasn't doing what I was supposed to do. Finally, when I went back to school, I dropped forever my dream of being a dancer." Again, sadness clouded Phyllis's face.

"When we work together again," I said, "it is important that we go back into your adolescence and we talk to those parts of yourself that have been living without nourishment all this time. You also live with a very strong male shield, Phyllis. You're a very beautiful woman, but you hide that beauty, and I think somehow that your feelings of feminine quality are wrapped up in your ability to dance. That's part of what you have shut down, isn't it?"

"Yes, it is. The feminist movement made me very angry. I didn't like the feminist movement. I sided with my husband against all of that, feeling that it was a denial of the power of woman rather than a regaining of the power of woman."

"I think it would be very wise for you, Phyllis, to reread some of those feminist books from the past. I'll give you a list. Understand with renewed vision what women have tried to do. There is no question that we have made enormous mistakes, and I think perhaps the most glaring flaw in all of the feminist work is that there was a great lack of sacredness, and if we did find sacredness, we put it outside ourselves in a goddess or god. We didn't take that goddess inside and realize that we are that goddess. But that is significantly changing now. You, Phyllis, are that goddess. When we heal that adolescent time inside you, I think you will find that your hot flashes will go away and your hormones will come into balance. There are a lot of herbs, too, that I can introduce you to. I'm not telling you to take anything; I'm just saying you might enjoy exploring this whole new world of energy and see what fits and what doesn't. Do you have terrible cramps from time to time, Phyllis?" I asked.

"Yes, I do."

"I'd like you to try something at home when cramps come.

Visualize the unborn dancer within you, trying to have life, to be born. See yourself giving birth to this dancing part of yourself."

"Will this help my cramps?"

"I don't know, but maybe. Be sure to keep a journal about your experiences from now on. Call me if you need me. I'll be in town for several weeks," I said as I walked her to the door. I gave her a copy of *The Power Deck* to use at home as a tool to center herself and to help her work with her private world of spirituality. I also lent her a drum to use until she could get one of her own.

RIDING THE FIRE

~~~~~~~~~~~~~~~~~~~~~~~~~~~~

THE ALCHEMY OF HOT FLASHES

~~~~~~~~~~~~~~~~~~~~~~~~~~~~

"Ride with me."

Woman at the Edge of Two Worlds beckoned me to follow her.

"Ride the fire when it enters your body. Centuries ago woman held the power on earth. She knew the alchemy of heat would purify her body and change her forever into a being of power. The heat is the source of your new life. Some do not need the fire in their bodies. They can still ride me into the land of their dreams."

10

RECAPITULATION

I sat at a table in a restaurant in Beverly Hills. La Famiglia had been there for years. I remember dining there with an old friend of mine when I first met Agnes Whistling Elk. My friend, a playwright, had encouraged me to return to Agnes in Canada. "Dissolve into nature," he had urged. I was finding it difficult to merge creation with life. I realized that I was still finding it difficult. I remembered I had wondered at the time if I was too old to so drastically change my life. I was thirty-something at the time.

I sat this evening with several friends, white table cloth over a pad, silver and crystal goblets of water and wine in front of us. The low lights were reflected artistically in the smokey glass around the room. It was a small, elegant restaurant. We all ordered different kinds of pasta, laughing, talking about politics and the events of the day. I was wearing a black wraparound dress. I secretly surveyed my reflection in the mirror. I had just washed my hair, and even though it had lost some of its shine through this process of menopause, I still had a healthy tumble of blond curls to my shoulders. I thought of Sally, my dear friend, who, when she had hit forty, cut off her beautiful, thick hair to her jaw line. She had said, "Older women shouldn't wear long hair. It drags your features down, you know." I looked at my reflection and wondered if my longer hair was dragging my features down or not. It didn't seem to me that it was. I remembered seeing little old ladies when I was a child with Cupid-bow red lips and dots of pink rouge on their cheekbones. I wondered if I just wasn't seeing as well as I used to. I tossed my head with a sigh.

Sandy asked me to pass the butter. Looking at me a little quizzically she said, "You know, Lynn, I don't know why you're writing a book about menopause. I've been in menopause for two years and the change of life has not changed my life at all."

Taking a sip of wine and putting the glass down, I looked at my friend and said, "Gee, I had no idea you were going through menopause. You never mentioned a thing to me."

"Well, there was nothing to tell," Sandy said. "I have just breezed through this. There was just no big deal."

Sandy was wearing a low-cut dress, a little too low, with her breasts bulging voluptuously. She looked beautiful. Her husband, a successful artist, was obviously proud of her, but there was a sense of subtle desperation about her, something that I had noticed for the last couple of years, but I hadn't really thought about it much. I looked at her again and saw that her face was damp, even though the restaurant was filled with air conditioning. I was actually cold, and I'm usually warm. I thought, "Right, Sandy, right," as I looked at the beads of perspiration on her forehead. If only we could be truthful to ourselves about what's in our minds, if we could find the courage to share that, then a unity of knowledge could be found.

"Really, Lynn, I always get warm when I eat," she said, watching me watch her as I ate a forkful of salad.

"Great. I think that's wonderful, Sandy. I wish that I could say the same. It's been more difficult for me."

Judy, a woman forty-five years old, brunette, sylphlike, tall, and lovely, was sitting at the end of the table with her longtime boyfriend. Her boyfriend was maybe eight years younger than she. "Hey, do we have to talk about old people subjects?" she said. "Allen and I are going to have children, you know."

I looked at her wide-eyed, knowing that she was forty-five, although she looked thirty-five.

"I know of a lot of women who have children at forty-five, even at fifty," she said.

"Yes, there are many menopausal pregnancies," Sandy said. "I've heard about that. I don't know why anyone would want to have children in their middle forties, quite honestly, and especially for the first time."

Judy was quite affronted by her statement. She took a sip, more like a swig, of wine and set the glass down rather hard so it spilled a bit. "Well, why don't we talk about something else." I felt an emotional curtain drop in front of her.

This was an uncomfortable subject for both of the women sitting at the table. Then I realized with a pause that it was just as uncomfortable for me to discuss, especially with my boyfriend present. In fact, if I were honest with myself, I didn't want to talk about this either. Who brought it up anyway? I had to laugh. I thought, See—this is exactly why so little research has been done about this subject. Women would rather down a brandy snifter full of poison than admit to being in menopause.

Finally I voiced my opinion even though I knew I was going to be very unpopular. "You know why the medical profession has not researched menopause more fully? Again, we want to blame doctors, but I think we have to take some responsibility. Really, before now we have not demanded that we need to know more. We as women have just let it go by. What has happened is that there is very little known about this whole subject. Our generation is probably going to be the guinea pig. But as you say, girls, this is probably not a conversation for the dinner table. Maybe we can get together and talk. I would like to share what I'm writing about and what I'm trying to reveal that has not been seen before."

Just then the waiter came with beautiful plates of food, plates with cheese and pasta and tomato sauce. We forgot what we were discussing and began to laugh about the movie we had just seen about a famous woman actress being impersonated by a man. Our long friendships served us well. No one seemed to notice that our laughter was a little louder and our conversation a little more exaggerated than usual.

II

BETH

Beth and I were walking in a lush, green meadow, the mustard grass coming up to our waists. The sun was warm behind occasional thunderheads. It had been a long and unusually wet spring for Los Angeles. Beth watched me out of the corner of her eye, her gaze averted down to the grass and the flowers. I sensed in her a tenuous quality, and I smiled to myself, remembering how I similarly had approached my teachers in the past. Beth had been working with me as an apprentice for a year now. She was a tall, blond woman, her naturally blond hair tethered back in a ponytail. Beth was a very kind and giving person, so generous that she had given her power away to almost everyone in her life. To please her family and take care of an ailing father and mother in their elderly years, she had not gotten married until she was thirty-four years old. I watched her as she picked some tiny fiddle-neck flowers, sniffing them, holding them close to her heart.

"Your innocence," I said, "makes you very good for this work."

She looked up at me with a big smile and handed me the flowers. "I've always been too trusting," she said. "Everybody laughs at me. When I was younger, they even called me stupid. I've always trusted people; I don't know why."

"You trust people, Beth, because you trust your own heart. You know about caring for others. You are so open. You're not afraid to learn something new. That's why I enjoy working with you so much."

We walked on down to the sacred circle of stones by a tiny stream that ran with water as long as the rains continued. A white egret with long, sticklike legs sat in the tree above us, a visitor from lands farther north.

"That egret is not unlike you, Beth. Tell me what you see in that bird and how it is similar to you." I found myself taking on the blanket, or shaman mask, face of my spiritual teachers, and I couldn't help but witness myself in the dance of life and how things come around full circle if one but sees with awareness.

Beth sat at the perimeter of the sacred circle. She raised her left hand, honoring the guardians of the circle. She sang her power song in clear melodic tones. Her voice floated on the wind that had come up from the west, carrying the scent of ocean spray and fresh spring fragrance. I sat next to her and a little behind her so as not to disturb her thinking and to lend her strength. She looked at the bird for a long time. The egret lifted its wings once and thought better of flying away. She watched us with some suspicion, making sure that we meant her no harm.

Beth turned to me after a short time, and said, "It is perfect, isn't it. It's a true sign. That egret is so much like me as it tried to test its wings, to move out, to make an act of power, and thought better of it. How many times I have done that in my life! I wanted to marry so much earlier, but I was afraid to rebel against my family rituals. My responsibility was so enormous with my family, and they made sure that I felt it. They wouldn't let me go, and now I have found my mate. I am happy, so happy, and we want to have children, but I am in menopause, early menopause. How could that be? I feel like that bird in the tree, a solitary figure of white, pure, against the barren branches. Somehow I feel that if I take flight, I will lose my way, that I will not be safe."

She looked at me, her beautiful blue eyes filled with tears. I reached out to hold her hand, wishing that Ruby were here to do some antic, some craziness, that would move Beth into laughter and out of her place of self-obsession. It is the process of movement from one state of being to another that enlightens us. Ruby had done that with me all these years with Agnes, and I understood now more fully why shamans work in the way they do. It is almost too much for one person to handle, but it can be done, and Agnes had taught me well.

"Stand, now," I said. She stood up suddenly, responding to the strict focus in my voice, lifting her eyes up off the ground with surprise. "Now, run toward the tree and flap your arms," I ordered.

She did so, making a commotion, and the egret, not wanting to move from its comfortable branch, lumbered up out of the tree and flew away, squawking, bleating its song of confusion. Beth turned to look at me. She had confusion in her own eyes. I said nothing. She looked at me, wanting an explanation.

"Why did you make me frighten her?" she asked.

After several minutes, I said, "Sometimes fear is a good thing," purposely not giving her further explanation.

I looked at her a while longer as wind came up again along the ground, ruffling the grass into waves of green, swirling around us in an eddy and then dispersing. I enjoyed the wind playing with us for a few minutes. The west wind has always been a strong ally of mine. I held my hand out softly, feeling her underneath my fingers. She always told me when things were right or when I needed to be aware. I took a deep breath, cocking my head, unable to help the smile lifting the corners of my mouth. I could see myself years ago, standing there in Beth, full of confusion and slight anger.

"Fear is a great motivator. None of us like to be in fear, but there are times when it makes us move. It makes us move when we're stuck."

Beth thought about that for awhile. Finally, she took a deep breath, nodded her head, and sat down in the grass. I sat down across from her. "You're right, my teacher," she said. "If I had not been afraid, I would never have moved out of the situation with my family. I moved because I feared the loss of my life. I would never have moved toward marriage. I understand what you are saying."

"Yes, Beth, this life is a perfect mirror. We do not see those mirrors, however. Menopause is another mirror for you. It creates a mirror that you cannot avoid looking in. It's out of your control, just as the egret could not control you running toward her. There's nothing you can do about it. Yes, you are losing your fertility, but perhaps you are not meant to have children in this lifetime, so now you have to give birth, a birth of a different kind, within your own spirit. Your life now is with your husband and with the Great Spirit that lives within you. Now you will have to face what you have really come here to do."

I pulled a piece of grass and sucked on the sweet tender end, looking away from Beth, looking out across the meadow with its own kind of virginity. It was fenced and refenced, these acres, with NO TRESPASSING signs everywhere. The land was owned by a man who never came to see it, but wanted it as a good investment. He had fenced the land to keep people out in case he'd be sued. He allowed one small gate on a friend of mine's property. It was through that gate that I came out in this meadow and blessed it every time I could.

"Even this land resembles your life, Beth, the fertile mother, Mother Earth, magnificent, unable to give forth its blessing except to the sky, because she is fenced. There are signs keeping everyone away, signs of treachery, fences of consciousness that have held situations, opportunities, at bay. Do you see what I'm saying, Beth? You have often said to me, 'If only I could work with Agnes and Ruby. If only I could know the Sisterhood.' Don't you see that everywhere there are teachers? Everywhere there is a Red Dog and a Ruby and an Agnes. This field of spring beauty is Agnes and Ruby. You could say that the fence, in a way, is Red Dog, a fence around your consciousness if you allow it. But you are free to fly across the earth, the fences, the fertile valleys, like the egret, if you can find the motivation to do so. Let yourself fly. Look deeply into the process of menopause, now, and see that it is a mirror of enlightenment for you. Sadness, yes, but I want to take you to the place where we can initiate you into your wise-blood. You are moving into your teacherhood, your time of wisdom as an elder, very early in life. Perhaps that means that it is your calling. Because so many women in recent history have missed an initiation with Woman at the Edge of Two Worlds, some women are being called early to walk through the lodge of wise-blood, because their wisdom is needed. What do you think?"

"You know, Lynn, the fear is a strange kind of fear, and it sometimes makes me paralyzed. Instead of flying off as the egret does, sometimes it makes me hold in terror to that barren branch, to a position that is not good for me. I'm afraid that I will not be good enough. I cannot imagine myself as a teacher of any kind." She looked down at the earth wistfully. Taking a stick, she began to draw in the earth, slashes, one after another, leaving little ridges of sand and moist earth.

"Fear is like grief. It deepens you, if you allow it. Take your consciousness into the deep, innermost part of your fear. Lie down in the grass, Beth, and close your eyes. Take a very deep breath."

I let her relax for several minutes. I looked up to the sky, and for a moment the clouds ceased boiling above us, turning into black and gray and gold-edged figures, ancient storm kachinas dancing in the northern wind that had come up suddenly down off the San Bernadino mountains, bringing the scent of snow and the taste of cedar and pine. I closed my eyes, and I thought of my teachers, their faces close inside me, smiling, giving me strength and encouragement.

"When you speak of fear, where do you feel this fear of not being able to have children in menopause? Where do you feel all of this in your body?"

Taking a deep breath, she followed her consciousness down into her heart. "In my heart," she said, holding her fists over her chest.

"Move with your consciousness into your heart," I directed, "holding the thoughts of your fear, of being paralyzed, not being able to move out into your acts of power. Tell me what you see inside your heart. What form does your fear take?"

"I see a giant black rock."

"Become that rock by saying 'I am.' Describe what you feel like."

"I am very large and my surface is smooth and I am very cold. I can't seem to move. I want to roll down the hill, but I can't move myself. Inside I am full of energy and I dream the most beautiful dreams. I want to write about them; I want to express them into the world, but I can't, because I can't move. I am a stone. I need someone to move me. I need someone to pick me up and take me where I want to go."

"Stone, where is it that you want to go?"

"I want to go up to the top of the hill so I can see out over the world," Beth said, her voice very faint and far away. She was very good at going into a deep trance, and I kept reminding her to breathe.

"If you go to the top of the hill, will that make things better?"

"Oh, yes it will."

"All right. Imagine, now, that I am lifting you up; I am lifting you to the top of the hill."

"Oh," Beth said, "now I can see out over the world."

"Is that now going to help you?"

She thought for a long time. There was a low rumble of thunder rolling through the valley. Still there was a warm undercurrent of air coming from the west, from the sea. Occasionally the sun was blotted out by the thickness, the density, of the thunder-clouds.

"It's interesting," Beth said. "It doesn't seem to help being up here. I want to move everywhere. I want to go everywhere. I want to travel around the world. I want to move. I feel like I can't move."

"Let's try something else," I said. "Let those images fade away and move more deeply inside yourself, inside the vast inner universe within you."

"It's a giant womb," Beth said almost immediately. "There's a blackness at first. I'm moving through infinite space. Now I see stars and the moon, so beautiful. I feel like I am in a womb, a universal womb, of darkness."

"Is that darkness bad?" I ask.

"Oh, no, it feels like velvet, almost like a cocoon," she said, a slight smile on her face, tears rolling down her cheeks.

"What is the sadness?" I asked.

"Oh, it is not sadness. I feel a relief as if suddenly my real womb has given birth to something."

"Can you describe that something?" I asked.

"I don't understand this," Beth said after several minutes. "I feel suddenly so at peace. I don't know that I have ever felt this at ease. I feel that I am floating in space."

"Stay with that."

I let her stay in that position of floating for a long time, and then she gave a deep sigh and began to sob, deep, heartrending sobs. I left her alone. I let her be in this very private space for some time. The soft west wind helped her in her dreaming and kept her warm and comfortable. The north wind seemed to have gone away. But I saw something in Beth that I wanted her to find on her own. Finally, I reached out, gently touching her on her arm.

"Where are you now, Beth?"

"I am far, far away," she said. "I feel like there is no limit to where I can go. I feel like I'm in the womb and that somehow I am the womb and that I'm moving over the earth, able to clarify my position. It is like I can be anything I want to be. Isn't that strange?" she said. "Suddenly I feel a release. How is that happening? I don't ever want to leave this place of peace."

"Take a deep breath, Beth, and let yourself go even deeper. I feel some fear, still, some tension around your solar plexus, around your place of shaman will and intent."

Taking a deep breath, she moved even deeper, and now a true smile came into her face. "Oh my god, I see something in the distance."

"What do you see?" I asked.

"I see a goddess figure. She is most resplendent. She is radiant. She is walking toward me on a beam of light." She went on with her dreaming, quiet for some time, and then her body started to jerk slightly. "Oh my god, oh my god," she kept saying.

"What is it, Beth?"

"I feel as if I am looking at the face of the Great Mother. She's smiling at me, Lynn, she's smiling at me." Tears were running down her cheeks. "She was young at first and now she is turning very old, still so beautiful. She's handing me something."

"What is it?"

"It looks like a bone, all beaded at one end."

"What are you feeling, Beth?"

"I've not spoken of this, but my legs hurt at night, and I think the bone is a leg bone."

"I know. I could see it. I wondered when you'd tell me. It can be part of menopause, Beth. You need to ask your doctor, but Bone Woman is telling you to take calcium. She is presenting more than that to you. Bone Woman gathers the bones throughout history. If you work with her, she will teach you how to heal your bones. Stay open to her."

"I will, Lynn. I will. I realize something that I never realized before this moment. I Am—I am the Goddess. It's as if I gave birth to this great being of light, and yet she has given birth to me. I see what my menopause is about. I really do see that."

I waited several minutes, and then, very gently, I asked her, "What do you see, Beth?"

"I see that I am a teacher and that somehow there's a lesson for me about bones. I see that I can work with elderly people and osteoporosis, because I understand them as well as anyone. I have lived with elderly people all of my life. My parents were fifty years old when I was born. I know my act of power, and it's as if I've given birth to that knowledge, and yet I see that the Great Mother has given birth to me. We're one and the same."

Suddenly there was a flutter of wings, and I looked up at the sky. The egret, white and snowy, was flying above us, and this time the egret was flying with another bird. As I watched them, I saw that they were obviously mates. They showed no fear of our presence, and again they landed in a tree not far away.

Beth took a deep breath. I told her to come back into her heart and to allow herself a chance to come back to the meadow. "Take as long as you need. Stay in the quietness and the stillness until you feel complete and at ease."

She took long, deep breaths as I had taught her and brought her consciousness back up out of her heart, up to her crown chakra at the top of her head, the highest place of energy in the body, and slowly began to breath normally and open her eyes. I sat behind her now and turned her face gently so that her first vision was the birds in the tree. As she looked toward the egrets, she caught her breath and smiled, then began to giggle. She sat up, shaking her head, smiling at me.

"I realize something, Lynn. There are many kinds of fertility, many kinds of births and rebirths in the world. I see what you have been telling me. I've experienced it now, so your dream can become my dream."

12

THE PATCH

It was the weekend and I needed to get out of the city. I met Bill at the airport in Phoenix and we drove north. It was a blistering hot day in Arizona. We had decided to stay with friends in the desert wilderness north of Scottsdale. Later that afternoon we were enjoying the saguaro cactus, scrub pine trees, and the beautiful sand-colored rocks that reminded me of some of the mesas that Agnes and Ruby and I had visited in Montana. We were sitting on large, flat sandstone boulders edging a natural spring that bubbled out from the side of a mountain. The desert lay below us, silent and strong beneath the waves of heat. I was slathering myself with 30 SPF sun protector. I turned to my friend and rubbed the thick cream on his back.

"Oh no," he said with a roguish smile. "I want to get tan. Don't put that stuff on me."

"Okay, Bill, but I need it." I put more on myself and handed the bottle to him. He squeezed out an ample amount and began rubbing it on my shoulders. Soon after, as the waterproof stuff dried on my shoulders and my back, I could stand the 115 degree heat no longer, and I walked carefully over the pine tree roots and slippery stones and slipped into the cool spring water.

"Mind if I join you?" Bill said as he slithered into the pool next to me.

I looked at his stout, once-handsome body as his protruding belly, hanging over his bathing suit, disappeared under the surface of the water. But I had trained my mind to think differently now. Instead of curling my lip in disgust at our failing white bodies, I switched my attention to his thick wonderful hair. I watched him watch me as I took an inflated rubber raft that he had brought for us to enjoy and tried to ease myself gracefully up onto it so that I could lie on my back on the rippling water. But as fate would have it, the raft kept slipping out from under me in one direction or another, until finally, I was splashing wildly, trying to get it between my legs so that I could at least ride it like a horse. With one of the slippery flailings, the raft flew several feet into the air and splashed down behind me. Bill started laughing uproariously. I looked down to readjust my bathing suit bra. Ever since I had been taking estrogen, my breasts had grown until now I looked like a powder pigeon in my bathing suit. Bill paddled his way over to rescue the raft and held it for me as I struggled up onto it. I'm in good shape for my age, I thought, but still, my skin just doesn't look the same.

"Why is it," I said to Bill, "that it has taken me so long to find friends with a pond I can swim in? It's something about my Piscean nature, I guess, that I love to swim and love to watch the reflections of the sky ever changing on the surface of still water."

"Yes," Bill said, "me too," in his usual quiet style.

For several minutes he hung onto the raft as I floated on it. Bill and I had been together for a couple of years now, but I was still nervous about wearing a bathing suit and displaying my body in bright sunlight. Ugh! My nervousness was not because I wanted to get married or didn't want to get married or because I was trying to make some kind of impression. It was just that I was shy about what was happening to my body, even though at times, I was fascinated by those changes. Suddenly there was an odd sparkle on the water. I averted my gaze from the sun, shading my eyes, and caught sight of something flat in the water that was reflecting the light in a kind of dimpled fashion.

What is that? I said to myself, staring. With a gasp I realized what it was, and I reached back to my hip with the palm of my hand, swinging my arm and my shoulder around, flopping myself off the inflated raft face down in the water. I reached out for the little floating disk, madly trying to catch it before it was seen by my boyfriend.

Bill, watching me, not understanding what was going on, asked, "Lynn, what is the matter with you?"

"Oh, nothing," I said, patting around on the surface of the water with my flattened palms, looking for the little disk, which of course was my estrogen patch.

Finally, as I searched and searched, I turned around to hear Bill say, "Is this what you're looking for?" He held the little transparent circle up to the sun.

"Oh, yes, that's it," I said.

"Well, here it is," he said. "What in the heck is it anyway? It's an odd thing to be wearing in the water. A new kind of bathing suit?" He laughed.

"Not funny," I said as I got out of the pond and toweled myself off with a turquoise, purple, and pink bath towel that said Hawaiian Tropic on it in bold terrycloth letters. I rubbed my hip until it was thoroughly dry, took the disk, patted it carefully, and placed it back on the little red patch on my hip.

"Gee, I've never noticed that before," Bill said. "What are you doing anyway? Did you cut yourself?"

"No, it's an allergy test that my doctor wanted me to have."

"Allergy test? Come on, Lynn, you don't have allergies," Bill said, holding his head to one side, a quizzical look in his eye.

"Oh, damn. It's my estrogen patch," I admitted.

"Estrogen patch? What do you mean?" he said.

"Well, when you go through menopause, sometimes people take estrogen."

"Oh, that's good. I didn't know they had it in a patch. I

thought you took it in a pill," he said, instantly disinterested.

"Well, this is a new way to have estrogen replacement, and it is pretty good, except that I seem to be allergic to the adhesive underneath it."

"In that case let's take it off and forget the whole thing."

"It isn't as easy as that. I wish I could, but it seems to be important for me to have this," I said.

"Why?" he asked, holding the raft between his arms and floating half in and half out of the water as he did so.

Later that evening as Bill and I sat on the porch of my friend's house, looking out at the sunset, I took a sip of my light beer and raised the glass to him.

"Skoal," I said. "Here's to no more denial."

"I'll drink to that," he said, lifting up his glass of beer as well. We clinked our glasses and took a sip. "What do you mean denial?"

"Well, that little incident in the pool today—"

"Yes." Bill laughed a bit at my reticence to bring up the subject.

"I realize that I thought today, on some reactive primal level, that if you saw that patch, you wouldn't love me."

"What?" Bill said. "That is absolutely crazy."

"Is it?" I asked. "You know, you and I have never discussed age. We have just kind of gone along not worrying about all those things—bodily functions and all that. But you know I was very surprised at myself. I was scared to death to have that patch floating around on the surface of the water. I thought it was like a little shield with symbols all around it, saying Lynn is over the hill, Lynn is losing her turf to younger women, and Bill is going to pick up that shield, maybe not physically, but certainly in his heart and in his mind, and he's going to think, 'I need to be shielded from Lynn, because she is too old for me. She's too old for me to be interested in her any more. I'm glad I found this little shield.'"

Bill looked at me with astonishment, his mouth dropping open a bit as he stared at me. "Don't you trust me more than that, Lynn? Are you really serious? I can't believe you're saying this, and P.S.—you're younger than I am."

"Well, I can't believe I'm saying this either," I said. "I can't believe that I'm saying something that is basically so insecure, but do you know, I've got to be honest. I really mean it. I felt that, and I also feel very foolish in admitting it. So what do you think?" I asked finally, as he stared at me in a long silence that made me even more uncomfortable with the subject.

"You know, age means nothing to me, chronological age, but I do hope that we have many long years together. What does mean something to me is integrity, trust, and honesty. There is nothing about me and my life with you that needs to be hidden," he said.

"And there is nothing about my life that needs to be hidden, except what is secret and sacred with me and my teachers. What I have learned from you, Bill, is that I can relax and trust what is real and truthful. But you know, I have learned all of my life to hide age and to hide anything that might upset the men in my life. I learned that very early from my father. If I upset him, he would hit me, so it has been ingrained in me since day one, and it's a hard thing for me to unlearn, very hard."

"I really do understand," Bill said, and he reached over and gave me a big hug.

"Thank you for understanding this, for not being disappointed with me," I said. "You know, I think it's important for my sisters in this world and for myself to know about the passage of menopause in a much more intimate and powerful way."

"I think that's true," Bill said. "My mother had a very difficult time when she went through the change of life. She was hospitalized at one point."

"Did they tell you why?" I asked.

"They didn't say why, but you know, after this experience with you today, I would imagine it was a very lonely passage for her. I don't remember having ever talked to any woman about menopause."

"Of course not. Most women would rather take cyanide than admit to being in menopause. And yet, every woman goes through it," I said. "Do you see what I'm saying, Bill? People don't admit some of the more powerful and important passages of life. Little girls don't talk about getting their periods. Older women certainly don't talk about menopause, because it is verboten in some way. It is something that you hide, that you don't display. But when hormones shift and change, there is a tremendous reaction in the body. Estrogen alone governs three hundred or more functions in the body."

"It does?" Bill asked with amazement.

"Yes, and there has been so little research, Bill. I have gone to my gynecologist and he says, 'Well, it's kind of your call. You can balance your body with herbs and homeopathics'—which incidentally, worked pretty well for me—'or you can take estrogen replacement therapy, but if you do, you might heighten the chances of getting breast or uterine cancer. We don't know. We hope not, but we don't know.' Isn't that wonderful? Now that we have reached menopause—fifty million women are going into menopause in the next ten years—there is still very little information about what happens."

"Wow," Bill said, sitting back in his chair. "I imagine that's true, isn't it. I wonder why there has been no research?"

"Well," I said, watching the orange and purple streaks in the sky as the sun began to set over the desert, "I think that women haven't demanded it, for one thing. Second, I've been told that the medical profession didn't see any money in the subject of menopause except for yanking out your uterus in often times unnecessary surgery, perhaps because you were bleeding too much. When I began menopause I would bleed, as women often do, very profusely, and what my doctor did for me was to balance the ratio of androgens and hormones. I bled off and on for six months after my gynecologist gave me a shot of progesterone for birth control. It wasn't until months later that he got my hormones back in balance and I finally quit bleeding. Most women by that time would have had a hysterectomy. I didn't even realize progesterone was a hormone. That was partially my fault because I didn't ask enough questions, but you know how doctors are. They get really busy and they don't want to hear your questions, and they get irritated that you asked the questions in the first place. But it's your body and it's your life, and no one is going to take responsibility for that except for you."

"Amen," Bill said, taking another sip of beer.

"But this passage of menopause not only marks a change in the way you deal with your own health, but it has to do with how you look at your aging process," I said.

"It's perplexing," Bill said.

"Men go through male menopause," I said.

"They do?"

"There have been new studies in England where they do implants of testosterone just under the skin and it releases for three months a certain amount of testosterone every day. Men who start losing their testosterone become irritable and gloomy. Their libido is almost absent. People's marriages begin to break up. It's not unlike what happens to women when they get close to menopause or their periods.

"You know, Bill, when I was sitting in the hospital with Mother when she was dying, I went into early menopause, into violent menopause. I was hot, cold. With almost every breath that my mother took, my temperature would change. I thought I was fainting. I had no idea that I was in menopause."

"But with all your training, why did you need to be told?" Bill wanted to know.

"I was in a state of denial with my mother's death. I refused to comprehend or honor my own reality. So, if you find yourself with your moods changing and your libido waning and you are not interested in sex, instead of blaming it on your partner"—I laughed and poked him with my elbow,—"you might consider having a blood test to check your testosterone levels."

"I guess that's probably a thought, isn't it?" he said, reaching over and giving me a kiss on the cheek. "But for now, that doesn't seem to be a problem," he said with a smile.

Quietly, we both turned to look at the golden sun setting behind the desert mountains. Streaks of gray, pewter-colored clouds streaked the azure sky. It was a beautiful evening, an evening of tranquil peace and serenity. I took a deep breath and gave thanks for my friends and for the wonderful people in my life who I care so much about. The sun sped toward the horizon, becoming more intensely golden with every moment. Suddenly, as it disappeared behind the jagged sawtoothed mountains in the distance, the horizon was illuminated with a sharp edge of sur-real light not unlike the stark sense of the passage of time that I felt deeply within my own heart.

DANCING THE FIRE

~~~~~~

LIVING WITH MENOPAUSE

~~~~~~

Woman at the Edge of Two Worlds sat next to me, sparks of pure energy flying from her eyes.

"You are facing now the next half of your life. You are wise-blood, holder of power. You dance the fire now, sister. You celebrate what you have become."

13

COMFORTING THE SPIRIT

I flew through a storm over Arizona on my short journey back to Los Angeles. Lightning split the sky and the plane bumped and dove through the clouds. It was a frightening flight, everyone sitting belted to their seats, their knuckles white and shaking as they held the armrests with their hands. After half an hour of storm, the pilot flew above the clouds through thunderheads edged in golden light, black, billowing, boiling clouds, tumultuous beneath us. We flew up into the blue sky of early afternoon as if nothing had happened. As suddenly as the storm had been upon us, we were out on the other side, placid, streaking toward Los Angeles with a tail wind.

I sat back in my seat and took a deep breath. All my life I had fought off sea sickness and air sickness. I took two more ginger pills. Agnes had told me long ago that ginger settles your stomach, and it does. I felt the seat against my back and the support of the seat beneath me. I felt secure once again and laughed to myself as I thought how everything in life seemed to symbolize my passage with Woman at the Edge of Two Worlds. What a gateway this is! I said to myself. I thought that yes, indeed, it is like flying through a storm. You don't know when you're going to come out on the other side, and you don't know exactly when you entered the storm, but suddenly the ride gets bumpy and the thunder of unrest and confusion rocks your soul. And now suddenly out on the other side, you are in a pleasant day, and it seems as if you had been in a bad dream. I thought to myself of Twin Dreamers, who with her extraordinary sense of humor puts me in touch with my own truth. I remembered Twin Dreamers patting her belly. I got flashes of Buddha's belly and my teachings in Nepal with Ani. Again, I sighed and thought about how very much alike all teachings are, whether you are Buddhist or Hindu, Native American or Irish. The teachings of the spirit are really one teaching. Sometimes they are aimed at the heart and more applicable to your emotions, and sometimes more applicable to your mind. Certainly in the Western world, because we speak a more pragmatic language called English, we have a society that has grown out of the language that we speak. It tends to be materialistic, and very little of our life seems to be spent on the pursuit of spirit and the comfort of soul.

I had decided before I left Agnes the last time that I would go home and comfort my body and in turn my own spirit. Even though I was feeling wonderful and full of strength and excitement for what I really saw as a new perspective on my life, I knew that still in all, my body and my spirit together needed new comforting. I had decided that I was going to paint my bedroom a little different color, that I was going to bring light into my bedroom, using the color yellow, and soft throws of pink and lavender. I was going to plant new flowers in my garden, the colors of spring, red and pink fuchsias and bougainvillea, and yellow daisies for hope. Yellow has always represented hope and the strength of my will to me.

I lay back in my chair and reclined the seat. Closing my eyes, I did a practice that Agnes taught me very early on, which certainly has been used by everyone throughout the centuries who knows anything about the workings of the mind. I pictured, as I often do when I go to sleep at night, things that I am going to do the next day. I pictured how I am going to do them and what I am going to accomplish. It helps me greatly to move out of a state of confusion and chaos that my own emotions have so often put me in.

In my mind's eye I saw my bedroom, and I imagined taking off the sheets and putting new sheets in place of them in a lilac color, soft and soothing to my eyes. I have a very heightened sense of touch, so I decided that I would get a throw that was not made out of wool, but made out of fibers that were very soft and gentle to my fingers. Because I don't type or use a computer, I like to lie on my bed and write in longhand. I lie on my bed often and write my books. Instead of slipping under the covers, I cover myself with a throw. I decided that would be soft and comforting to me. I decided to use some of the sacred herbs that the Sisterhood had given me with lavender and sea salt. Then I would make, perhaps, a very beautiful urn to place by my tub, so that when I took my baths and cleared my energy field of positive ions, I would use this urn. I would make a little ceremony of the using of sea salt and herbal flowers. I thought that it would be wonderful to give this to my sisters, to share the ceremony that I had learned so well from Agnes and Ruby. I imagined myself drawing warm water, dimming the lights in my bathroom and lighting a white candle, opening the window next to my bathtub and listening to the birds, and giving myself an unheard of half an hour in the morning just to enjoy my bath. I would turn off the phone and enjoy nature and the spirits of my house and my garden that I had tended all these years.

I suddenly realized that the spirits around my house were trying to give me comfort, but I, because I was so busy, so rushed, always feeling urgency to finish this and that, never allowed myself time to give my own spirit comfort. So I divined for myself a different course of action, and I saw myself lying in the tub, comfortable, happy, smelling the scent of lavender steaming up from the water. Then I decided to get new towels, towels that were fluffy with a deep nap, just two or three towels and face cloths with new colors. I would go shopping for myself for once

and find something that really suited me, that did not decorate
my bathroom, but suited me and my senses. I thought with a
deep breath that I deserve it; all women deserve it, particularly at
this time in life. The health of the spirit is not separate from the
health of the body.

As we sped toward Los Angeles, I noticed it was getting dark
now. We were flying into the setting sun. It was like a long twi-
light, the sun becoming more and more orange on the horizon as
slowly it descended. Up ahead I could see a bank of smog and I
knew we must be nearing Los Angeles. How sad, I thought, the
city of the angels, a most magnificent city—how we as human
beings not understanding, not caring, not giving ourselves the
time for consciousness, have all but destroyed a beautiful city,
leaving it without aesthetics, without even a human flow of
energy. In some ways it was an inhuman place to live, and yet it
was my home.

Then I saw Agnes's face in my mind's eye, smiling at me, as she
had, not long ago, as we sat on a log in the horse pasture near
her cabin. "If you are a sacred being," she had said, "it does not
matter what you do or where you live. All that matters is how
you live, because sacredness is part of balance. If you can live,
Lynn, in Los Angeles and maintain your balance and the purity
of your spirit, you can live anywhere. It is very much easier to
live in a protected monastery as a monk in the Himalayas and
remain spiritually balanced. It is very difficult to have one foot in
the physical manifestation of a chaotic city and to keep the other
foot firmly implanted in the land of healthy spirit. It is one of the
reasons I have sent you there," she had said, drawing symbols in
the dirt with a long stick. "I sent you there because it is the people of the cities who need to be healed. It is the people of the
cities who lose their souls first, and yet, they are the ones who
make the decisions for the rest of society. They're the ones whose
faces you see on TV every night. They're the ones that people
tend to believe, even if they lost their souls long ago. So it is in
the cities that you need to work."

The vision of her face faded from my inner screen. The next thing I knew we were landing in Los Angeles. I felt the wheels touch down on the runway and bump a couple of times. I felt stronger and better than I ever had in my life, and I looked forward to working with my apprentices. I looked forward to the ceremony of initiation that we were soon to perform together in the high desert of California.

14

MARY

The next morning I sat with Mary, who had been my apprentice for many years. I knew she had always dreaded the change of life. We sat together in a stone circle on the hill behind my house in Los Angeles. The grass near the circle was pressed down to the ground in hollow indentations where a family of white-tailed deer had slept the night before. I passed the talking stick to Mary. The talking stick had been used by Agnes and me for years during our teaching process. It was a beaded cottonwood branch about two-feet long. It had many sacred bundles and feathers hanging from it. There were certain symbols painted on one side that represented the power of woman, the power of the sacred dream. Mary held the stick as she sat cross-legged on the ground. Her face was remote, her eyes cast down.

"I am feeling," she finally said, "as if the rug has been pulled out from under me. I am the same person who is working hard in her life as a psychotherapist to keep everything together, and yet all of a sudden, my own body seems to be working against me. I have no control over what is happening to me. With all I know about the mind, I seem to know nothing about my body. I had the same feeling when I gave birth to my child. Suddenly my body was giving birth to this baby two months early, and whether I wanted it early or not, it was going to happen. Similarly, I feel panicked and out of control. When my periods came a year or so ago with such heavy bleeding, I was frightened. I didn't even know what was happening to me. My doctor said there was something wrong with me; it must be stress. Now my periods have stopped and I miss my monthly visitor. I miss the cleansing and the assurance that I am still fertile."

She handed the talking stick back to me, obviously wanting my response.

"It is difficult when we feel things are out of control, Mary. But if you feel you are out of control it means, perhaps, that there is an issue of trust here. Perhaps you need to go back to thoughts of origin and the beginnings of life and the Great Spirit that animates you."

I passed the talking stick back to her. She thought for several minutes, running her fingers along the polished edge of wood grain between the circles of beading. "It's fear, Lynn. I wake up in the morning and before I can think, I am filled with terror. It's as if I'm facing an abyss and I don't know what to do." Tears rolled down her cheeks. "I feel so fragmented. I've lost my turf, like the core of my life is slowly being taken away."

"Core?" I asked.

"Yes, that place inside me where I have always felt my strength. I guess it's related to my feelings of sexuality, of being sexual."

"Is that so important to you?"

"Yes, it's part of my identity. I hate to admit it, but I've always been sexy and I enjoy the power of being beautiful, attractive. Now I feel like I'm losing my power, and I'm afraid. I don't know who I am anymore."

"But, Mary, menopause doesn't change your beauty."

"Menopause means that I'm over the hill. I don't want to be called an elder. I want to be sexy and young. Is that so terrible?" Mary began to sob uncontrollably in my arms like a terrified child. After a while she gathered herself together.

"Perhaps, Mary, it would help you to think about your god, the Great Spirit. Think about the life force that has always been there for you. Has it not? Can you find that place of trust?"

She took the talking stick and her face brightened a little. "Yes, Lynn." She took a deep breath and blew her nose.

"Feel your center, Mary."

She laid the talking stick down on the earth. "I need to have a conversation with you," she said. "May we do this?"

"Of course, but first close your eyes, Mary, and take a deep breath." She did so. I could see that her muscles were visibly tense. "Now, where do you feel your center in your body?"

"In my head," she barely whispered.

"Let's do an exercise that I learned from Shakkai, Woman of the Sacred Garden. Stand up and center yourself again, breathing deeply. Hold out your arm and with all your strength . . . Are you still centered in your head?"

"Yes," she said.

"Resist my pressure on your arm," I said.

I then pressed on her arm, pushing it down. The tension in her arm began to shake, and her arm gave way easily.

"I want you to remember the sense of weakness that you just had. Now, Mary, gently bend your legs a bit, and bring your consciousness, still with your eyes closed, down from inside your head to your shaman center around your navel area. Vividly stay there for a moment, breathing deeply and keeping your consciousness in that area of your belly. Then I want you to envision golden light emanating from that center up and out through your body, out through your limbs, down through your legs, and down through your arms—beautiful, radiant light. I want you to relax your muscles the best you can. Take another deep breath. Now I want you to raise your arm, not tensing, and with your elbow bent slightly, think of your arm as immovable. Keep your consciousness around your navel."

I reached out and tried to bend her arm and push it down. It was as strong as a large branch of a tree. There was no way her arm was going to move. Mary opened her eyes, stunned by the sense of her own strength.

"See. What you have just done is very simple. You have changed your focus from your mind to a place of power within you. You have reunited yourself with the oneness of the universe, the force of the earth that gives you life. Do you see that?"

"Yes, I do," Mary said. "I experienced a definite shift in my strength."

"Martial artists know about *chi*. That's where their abilities and strength comes from. It comes from being able to focus their energy in a certain way. Now if you would sit down again, Mary, and hold your consciousness still in that area of your body, I want you to think about the Great Spirit and your life. Think about your husband, how you love him, the difficulties you have. Where is your centeredness now, Mary?"

"It's back in my head again," she said.

"Do you realize how you went back into fear and lost your power?"

"Yes."

"All right. Move your consciousness back down around your shaman center, and think again about your husband and the problems you have. Always stay conscious on the periphery of your mind vision, the vision actually that is your body-mind. Still see that flow of golden light going out into your limbs and your entire body, renewing you with strength and power."

Mary took a deep breath. She began to breathe more easily. I could see more visibly that her muscles were beginning to relax. She stopped twitching her fingers and her facial muscles relaxed.

"Now that your consciousness is down where it's supposed to be, Mary, tell me about your fear."

Several minutes went by. A smile crossed her face gently. "Lynn, it's very interesting. When I think from my place of power in my belly, suddenly my fear seems to disappear."

"Do you understand why?" I asked.

"No, I'm not exactly sure," she said.

"Well, think about this. Perhaps when you move your mind down into your center of power, your trust is restored. It is restored, I think, for several reasons—partly because that's your place of power, and you're no longer lost in your head. The way I have learned the brain is part of the ego. The ego is always in conflict and fear, because it is always trying to defend itself. When you move your consciousness down into your shaman center, it is first of all an act of trust in itself. Then with the renewed strength that you feel, you begin to understand, almost on an unconscious level, that you have the capabilities of control over how you feel and act. You're not out of control. The defending of yourself means that you have the capability to fight for your own truth, that you stand for something, that you know beyond a shadow of a doubt that the life force is part of you and can never be separated from you, because you are that. You are the life force. If the body falls away in death, the life force goes on. You go on. So, you begin to witness the fact that you are made of power. You witness the fact that even though menopause occurs, it is the body changing and flowing onward in a life process, and the spirit can witness the entire drama from a position of equanimity."

Mary stiffened again. "But I don't like the process of death. I don't want to lose my father. I don't want to lose my family in this process."

I could see Mary getting tense again and moving her center up into her head. After several minutes I said quietly, "Close your eyes and imagine a river flowing in a mountain setting. Imagine beautiful mesas in northern New Mexico and snow-tipped mountains. It is springtime. Flowers are blooming in the meadows all around you. Watch the river flowing down from the mountains, the water reflecting the sparkling radiance of the sun. You're walking up along the river, gathering wildflowers to take to your daughter, and you're breathing in the spring air, the smell of northern snow on the wind. Is that a wonderful picture?"

"Oh, yes," Mary said, "it's wonderful. I love watching the water."

"What is it about the water that you like to see?"

She thought for several minutes. "Well, I like the way it reflects light from the sky and clouds, and I like the way that it is never-ending. There is a meadow that I go to in Montana that is at the foot of the mountains, and I always know that the water will be running there. It gives me a feeling of joy and security to know that, in a sense, the river water will always flow."

"Oh, really?" I said. "Is there anything in you that would want to stop the flow of that river?"

She thought for awhile. "No, Lynn, I can't imagine it."

"Don't you think that life flows in the same way, that there is an ebbing and a flowing, like the tides at the ocean shore, of life and life force and that always the force of life flows through us all throughout existence? We are really not separate. We are all one, you and I, just like single drops in the flowing water coming down from the mountains. Each drop becomes part of the greater whole. The river and the flow will go on forever. The water will eventually reach the sea. Then it will evaporate into the clouds, and again there will be rain and snow and the whole process will be started all over again."

Mary leaned back a little, the talking stick in front of her. She reached out and caressed the beads with her fingers as if reaching for security, something that was stable and real. "I never thought of it that way. Maybe it's true. It's a kind of trust, isn't it, Lynn? As you say, it's a trust that the water will always flow. It's a trust that when I go to sleep at night I will wake up in the morning. That's probably why a lot of people don't sleep very well, isn't it?"

"Yes, it is. It's a lack of trust—trust in what they are, trust in their own truth—their own trust in the deeper meaning of life."

She took a deep breath. "It helps me to envision life flow like that wonderful river that I love to sit beside in the summertime. It cools me and gives me such strength. Perhaps I can begin to witness life from a different position. Maybe now I can see menopause a little differently."

"Mary, don't ask too much of yourself. It's not that you change your feelings overnight, but it is true that we lose sight of why we're here. We truly do come onto this earth walk to become enlightened, and yet it is the one thing that we are most afraid of. Somehow enlightenment implies change. And that's true. It does, but in that change we are full of terror. When we are faced with something new, something that we have to shift and change to see more clearly, we are afraid to move. Menopause is a great mirror and a great gateway. The mirror consists of owning what we have created in life, of taking stock of who Mary is at this point. Part of the bridge between who you were and the new woman you are becoming is created by being grateful that you are still here, grateful for all that you have learned. The gateway is about moving your eyes in a different direction, the direction of spirit, of sacredness, of walking through the gateway with a new ability for expression, a new contact and relationship with your sacred will. All of these transitions will be symbolized in our ceremony with Woman at the Edge of Two Worlds."

Mary picked up the talking stick. She held it to her third eye and down to her lap. "You know, Lynn, I have always trusted that I would be cared for. When I have decided to do a project in life, when I went through the process of education to become a psychologist, I trusted that I had the power to do that, didn't I?"

"Yes, you did, and it was a tremendous effort."

"Yes, and that effort became so much easier because I had the trust that I could accomplish whatever I set out to do. It seems so strange to me now that I am suddenly filled with fear simply because I'm going through menopause, but I am. We sit here in ceremony together and I feel better. I can feel my consciousness moving back up to my head and I get rattled. It's like my consciousness is looking for something to be upset about. If I solve one fear, I look for another, and I can't help it. I'm still in a state of conflict."

"Mary, go back to your childhood for a moment. Close your

eyes and remember what the prevailing ambiance was in your home as a child. What was it? What did it feel like?"

"Well, tension," she said finally. "There was always tension, fear that I would do something wrong and somebody would be upset at me, that I wasn't good enough to be listened to. There was always conflict."

"And conflict," I said, "was something you learned that directly related to your survival."

"What do you mean?" Mary asked. She stroked her long hair that hung down over her breasts.

"I mean that you survived as a child, right?"

"Yes, I did."

"And in that survival was also a lot of conflict, right?"

"Yes," she said.

"Well, I can't imagine that your mind would do anything else."

"I don't understand," she said.

"You survived even though there was great conflict in your life. Therefore, I am sure somewhere in your unconscious you feel that to survive you must be in conflict."

"Oh," she said and thought about that for a while. "Yes, perhaps you're right."

"So, possibly your mind is looking for something to be in conflict about and has been taught through your own conditioning that to survive there must be some kind of tension and conflict. We need to change that. We need to teach you that that is no longer appropriate, and that in fact the conflict hinders your development. Is that not so?"

"Yes, it hinders my health; it hinders my ability to produce in the world."

"And probably, Mary, it is making you have tension and conflict about the passage of menopause, because somehow here you are frightened and you think you need to go into a survival mode. You know, Mary, it's probably like that crazy car of yours. You set the alarm on it and we go to lunch and the alarm goes off and there's nobody near your car. Right?"

She laughed. "You mean I'm constantly in a state of alarm?"

"That's right, even though you needn't be. It's like you're over-alarmed. It's an alarm system that goes off if there's a burglar, but there is no burglar. There is no one here to steal anything from you."

"Oh, but yes there is," Mary said. "My fertility, my sexuality, is being stolen from me."

"Oh, really? Remember the flow of the river and your sexuality hasn't changed. Remember the flow of the river," I reiterated.

"You're right." Suddenly Mary's face brightened. "You know what? In a way it's such a gift, menopause. I no longer have to deal with so many things that had to do with having my moon. If I could just relax into that fact!"

"That's right."

"And that in itself is an enormous relief." Finally, Mary's whole body relaxed. Tears of relief welled up in her eyes.

I lit incense from Mary's personal smudge bowl, a goddess bowl, given to her by a teacher in Greece, and spoke to it, fanning smoke to the powers of the four directions, honoring the Great Spirit, as the Sisterhood had taught me, the great Mother Earth, and the keepers of the bowl.

"Great Spirit," I said, "Mother Earth, great mothers who protect us and give us life, hear me now. This is a prayer for my sister Mary. This is a prayer for her wholeness, for her ability to create unity and power and understanding in her life. This is a prayer for her menopause. This is a prayer to Woman at the Edge of Two Worlds, for her to listen to my sister Mary and help her in this passage through the gateway of Changing Woman. She is a changing woman. She is a woman changing into the radiance of elder life. That is not a giveaway of life force, but a gaining of understanding wisdom and new life force. Help her to understand, great goddess, the difficulties along her trail. Help her to pick up the trail now, to live in a new position of power. Help her to stay strong. Great Spirit, Great Mother, I honor you and send you prayers of gratitude. I walk in beauty with you all the days of my life."

I turned Mary's goddess bowl to the four directions and held it up to the sky. I offered my prayers to Woman at the Edge of Two Worlds, and then I handed the goddess bowl to Mary. She smudged it with her favorite herbal blend, collected on the Isle of Corfu, and turning the bowl to the four directions, she took a pinch of herbs and held it up to the Woman at the Edge of Two Worlds.

"Great Goddess," she said, "Great Spirit, Mother Earth, my power animals, my ancestors, and all those who love me, hear me now. I thank you for this ceremony. I thank you for the sacred human teachers. I thank you for my life. I thank you for giving me the courage to see more clearly. Thank you, oh Great Spirit, for all that you have given me. Ho."

Mary held the goddess bowl up to the moon and then she said, "In celebration of my female truth and female consciousness in the world." She placed the bowl down on a special bag for it, embroidered with Greek symbols in bright blue thread.

15

BONE WOMAN: KEEPER OF THE BONES

I had a dream that night that Agnes and Ruby and the Sisterhood were gathering near Agnes's cabin again to do sacred ceremony, that something had happened with the families of some of the women of South America. It was very important for us to gather in a circle and do ceremony for them, to send them power. It had to do with some of the women from the rain forests and their land and their way of life being threatened.

In my work with the Sisterhood over these many years, I have learned that in a sense there is no time-space continuum when you move out of your body. You can receive messages through dreams and send messages through dreams. Learning can be transmitted from one continent to another. Shamans have been working in this way throughout history. For instance, when you look at knowledge from the Taoists in Asia, you find similar knowledge reflected in the Mayan lands. It is my understanding that shamans have communicated throughout human history on higher levels of consciousness. That is how, in my experience, we have been able as shamans and to understand one another. When I go to aboriginal Australia, I sit with the shamans there and we need not speak the same language. We understand one another instantly. It is in our eyes; it is in our energy fields. The source of power is always the same. It is from the firstness of woman, from our great Mother Earth, the original mother.

When I awoke that morning, I canceled my appointments and things that I was going to do, and I got on a plane and flew to meet with Agnes and several of the women from the Sisterhood of the Shields. I did ceremony with them and prayed for the healing of Mother Earth. We worked through the energy vectors and did our work as we have done throughout the centuries on this great schoolhouse that we call Mother Earth.

After two days and nights of ceremony, I went off with Agnes to talk and to work. We stayed out under the stars and found an aspen forest near the river that we had visited in the past when I was writing *Star Woman*. Ruby joined us after a day and we laughed and spent time with July. On this particular morning, before sunrise, Ruby and July went off to go fishing, something that both of them loved to do. Agnes and I went to do a sunrise ceremony and to pray together.

Agnes and I sat, watching the sun rise from a big tumble of rocks over by a canyon where we had done ceremony years ago with the celestial rattles when I had first met Agnes and Ruby. The sun came up from the east and we prayed together silently. Finally, Agnes, her face deeply tanned and framed by her long gray braids tightly wrapped with ribbon, broke the silence, her eyes watching me like a bird of prey looking for dinner. Immediately her intense gaze put me ill at ease. She surveyed me for some time as if she were enjoying my discomfort.

"How are you feeling?" she asked.

For a moment I didn't know quite how to answer her and I just simply told her the truth. "I feel intimidated, Agnes. Why are you looking at me that way? Have I done something wrong?"

"Why do you assume that because I am looking at you intently that you have done something wrong?" Her voice and manner were almost condescending. I was taken aback, struggling to maintain my center with my teacher.

"Well." I didn't know quite what to say. "I feel that I've made a mistake."

"Really." Agnes said. "Do you make mistakes often?"

"Well, no. Well, maybe sometimes I do."

"You don't sound like a woman of power to me," Agnes said, even more condescendingly.

"I don't think you're being very nice," I said.

"Well," Agnes said shrugging her shoulders, taking her gaze off of my eyes for a moment and looking toward the sky, which was now filled with golden-orange light from the rising sun. "Am I expected to be nice all the time?" she asked.

"No, I guess you're not. I just sort of hoped you would be," I said, trying a laugh to break the thickness of the atmosphere that had descended upon us, but Agnes did not laugh, which made me feel even more uncomfortable. She sat back in a position of animal power and strength, her eyes piercing into mine, as if she were about to pounce on her prey or her morning breakfast and tear it apart. "Look, Agnes, you're making me feel really uncomfortable. I wish you'd cut it out," I said, raising my voice a little. I couldn't imagine what she was doing, but I didn't like it.

"Oh," she said, "do you want to fight? Is that what this is all about?"

I shook my head, closed my eyes, and thought quickly back over the events of the morning, wondering what in the world had ticked her off, but nothing came to mind. "Look, Agnes, maybe I'm at a dead end street here or something. I don't know what I've done wrong. Obviously I've made you unhappy. Why don't you just tell me what's wrong?"

"Why do you assume that because I'm taking a stance like this with you that you have done something wrong?"

I thought about that for several minutes, and I looked at her and it dawned on me. "You know, I haven't done anything wrong, have I? And you're trying to provoke me. The minute you try to provoke me, I assume that I'm in the wrong."

"That's right, Lynn. You're giving your power away to me.

Why are you doing that? Why do women do that? Around the world, we as women give our power away, usually in the face of authority."

"That's right," I said. "Always when I was working within the patriarchal system as a stockbroker, for instance, my bosses were all men, and when anything ever happened, I was apologizing. You're right, Agnes. You're right, and I hate to admit it, because you really made me slip. But you know, whenever they came at me, taking out their frustrations on me, because I seemed to be the only woman around—"

"No, let me make a correction there," Agnes said. "You weren't just the only woman around; you were the only weak one around. It is something you see in nature, and when animals are running wild across the plains and the great forests of the world, survival of the fittest is one of the most important things. When the wolf goes to make a kill—let's just take the caribou for instance—the wolf will watch the herd for some time, looking for the weak ones. It's not only because instinctually it knows that's going to be an easier kill. It's also instinctually built into this great process called life. It's a process called survival of the fittest. Weak ones must be weeded out so that the strong caribou will mate and create even stronger caribou so that the species can survive. The wolf will watch its prey, and then it will go nip the heels of the caribou so that they bleed a little. The wolf might follow that caribou herd for a week, watching to see if that caribou is still the weakest. If that wolf discovers that the caribou is indeed the weakest, it will go in at last and make the kill. That sounds difficult, perhaps, but when you think of the larger vision of a species surviving, if the caribou herd breeds the weakest with the weakest, they will all die in the next few generations.

"As it is with people, we have denied our instinctual side. We don't recognize it, so often, when it comes up, but we tend, as a species, to go for the throat of those who are weakest. I think that a lot of that comes not only from social conditioning and wanting to be in competition and winning, making more money, being stronger materially, but it is also an instinct that when we see a weakness, and I don't mean a child that needs nurturing, but an adult, we will come in for the kill. So it isn't just because you were the woman, although I am sure that played a large part in the process that you experienced."

I sat, looking at my teacher for some time, wondering what this was all leading to, but knowing better than to ask at this moment. I knew that it would all be revealed to me. "You know, Agnes, you scare me when you move into a very male shield. You held up your shield as a warrior, and I was intimidated instantly. I backed into myself."

"Look at your body position," Agnes said, poking me with a finger, hard on my chest. I was rounding my shoulders, sitting slumped over.

"You're right. Look at me." Instantly, I pushed my shoulders back.

"No," she said, "imagine that from the stars above you there is a string coming down and attaching itself to your chest and pulling you up from the chest. Lift your chest up and out of it's cage. That's right," she said. "Then your shoulders fall back naturally. Don't force yourself into an unnatural position. You'll only get tired and go back to sitting the way you were before."

"You always sit so straight, Agnes. Why is it when people get older, they often hunch over? They lose their power in their bodies. I guess it's just aging, isn't it?"

Agnes didn't answer me for a long time. She glared at me. Finally, I thought about the words I had just spoken, and I started to shake my head.

"Yes, Lynn, shake your head, because you're wrong."

"Wrong about what?" I asked.

"There is a lot of talk in the world about bone loss."

"Osteoporosis," I said.

"Yes. What is that a symbol of to you?"

"Well," I said after thinking for a moment, "it's the structure of your body. It's the structure of your life, your support system.

When you lose your bones, you lose your structure and your support."

"That's right," Agnes said, "you no longer have a leg to stand on. Right? But it's the other way around. When you lose your intent, your will to structure your life, you lose bone."

"I'd never thought of it quite that way," I said.

"You lose your substance. A south teaching, a physical teaching about your relationship to substance. We assume as we get older that we are no longer young; therefore we can't do as much," Agnes said, standing up and twirling around on one foot. "I'm not supposed to be able to do this," she said, leaping into the air like a gazelle. "I'm old. I am really old," Agnes said. "I am older than time," she said, coming back to me and glaring at me as if she were wearing the mask of a clown. "I'm old and decrepit."

She leaped into the air, leaping over me. I whirled around to watch her, not really wanting her behind me without being able to see her.

"And you're going to be old real soon, too," she said, squatting down in front of me in the position that I, at my age, still found difficult after a few minutes. She seemed to handle it with great ease and agility. "You're going to be old, Lynn, and so is everybody else. You're going to be just as decrepit as I am. Then what? Are your bones going to fall apart? Are you going to be afraid to stand up for yourself, to fight back? Are you going to tell people when they're tearing you to pieces, 'I'm sorry. I must have been wrong'?" She was almost yelling at me.

There was a flame building inside me, a heat of anger, not only at her, but at myself.

"See," Agnes said. "Instead of getting angry at me, you're getting angry at yourself for not being stronger. Terrific, Lynn. You've learned to be a real warrior with us."

Now I started to cry.

"Oh, great," Agnes said. "Tears now. Woman's greatest weapon," she said.

I had to laugh as Agnes danced around in front of me. "All right, all right," I said, getting up and standing in front of her with my shoulders back and my head held high. "I see. I see what you're doing. You're just trying to make me mad."

Agnes took a big sigh. She reached out her hand and touched my shoulder and said, "Lynn, these shoulders carry the weight of the world. Women carry the weight of the world. It is a heavy weight, because from the day you were born, you knew how to *see*. You could *see* the pain in the world, and you wanted to do something about it. You cared. Women care. They want to nurture the earth back to health, but they're afraid to stand up for who they are. They've been taught their whole lives that if you are strong and powerful, you will lose your beauty and no one will love you, and we need to be loved. It's scary out there to be alone and everybody hacking away at you because you stuck your head up above the crowd, and you're special and you're different. That's you, Lynn. What are you going to do? Get scared? Hollow out your chest and round your shoulders so that your heart cannot love?"

I sat down in front of her, stunned by her vigilance. Tears stung my eyelids. I fought them back.

"That's right," Agnes said, "fight back your tears, because it's true, isn't it? You're scared. All of us women are scared, and the ones who get osteoporosis are more scared than others. They're afraid to take a stance, so their bones fall apart. They lose the calcium."

"But a lot of that, Agnes, has to do with genetics."

"Yes, but perhaps it's a lineage. Maybe it's a message that the entire family needed to learn throughout the history of incarnations of that family. It's something to look at," she said. "I'm saying it's a possibility and I want you to look at it carefully. Where's your killer, that being inside you that protects and fights for you? Where is she right now, Lynn? Where's that warrioress inside you?"

"Well, I guess she's hiding under that rock over there, Agnes."

"Yeah? Why don't you go find her. I'm going to give you a few minutes, Lynn, to go find her. I want you to move inside your killer, that warrioress. Take a minute. Bring her back here, and the next words I hear from you, I want them to be from her."

I closed my eyes and took several deep breaths and centered myself. I was more shaken than I realized, but I pulled my power back into my shaman center and I found my warrioress hiding under a rock inside myself. After a few moments I let her speak. "I'm the killer, Agnes. I'm the warrior inside Lynn, and I've learned how to fight. I know of what you speak. Lynn is too sensitive. She gets frightened and she gets scared. She gets terribly sad for how sisters do not stand together and fight for one another. If they don't understand each other, they don't try to communicate, they just turn a deaf ear and fight against one another. They will destroy each other. That's a tragedy that doesn't need to be, because women together can rule the world, and they can certainly heal the world.

"I need to be stronger. You see, Agnes, I'm Lynn's warrioress, and I'm really strong. I'm predatory, but I'm never allowed to fight unless Lynn loses her temper. Then I am formidable. Then I will fight for her, and she will survive, and she knows it. But she takes the weapons out of my hand. When I raise the sword, she takes it away. She'll let me carry the shield. She'll let the world know who she is. She has gone that far, and it's hard for most women to even do that. They are afraid to stand for who they are, but they're learning.

"But in old age I see the body is the greatest teacher, and Lynn is going to learn this. If you don't learn your lessons in early life, the body and Bone Woman, She Who Gathers the Bones, always win out. The body is your last teacher, in a sense. The body forces you to face what you have become, and if you are weak, the body becomes weak. As you are spiritually, you are physically. If you have not dealt with me, the killer, that warrioress inside, the shadow warrior is born, and the shadow warrior is that killer warrior inside that does not manifest when he is needed. That is the most important aspect of wholeness finally in the later years. When your bones start to disintegrate, it is because you don't take a stance, you feel no support, and structurally your life begins to fall apart, perhaps because you think you are no longer needed in your society. But if you are no longer needed, make a place for yourself where you are needed. There are many things that we can do in our older years. We are needed. The old wise ones are needed more in older life than ever. Society needs to be taught that again. Then you have the wisdom, you have lived, you have been down the trail, and you can point the way for younger women and men."

"You know what's going to heal the earth," Agnes said. "So structurally, if your bones are telling you that you need to pay attention to structure, that you need to pay attention to how you have ordered your life in a structural way, then do so. Don't give up. Don't round your shoulders and apologize for who you are. Take strength. Pick up your lance and move out into the world from a sacred stance, not from a place of anger, but know that the strength is in there. That 'killer' is alive and well. The warrior stands within you and announces to the world that you are not to be fooled with, that if they want to go into a position of harm with you, that you are worthy of harm, that you are a good enemy, and you will give them a good fight to the death, if needed. Then your bones will be healed."

I opened my eyes and looked at Agnes. Her eyes softened with kindness and compassion. She looked at me with great love in her heart, and she smiled for the first time. I took a deep breath. Thoughts were racing through my mind, and I realized the extraordinary truth in her words. I realized that in a sense the goddess is your body.

"Make an ally of Bone Woman," Agnes said. "She is the caretaker of your bones. Talk to her directly. Do ceremony with her. Light a candle for her. Go inside your bones with your consciousness and honor them for supporting you all these years. Your body is one of the greatest teachers of all, and when we enter spirituality as a true path in our life, we tend to throw our bodies away as if they are nothing. As we move through the gateway of menopause, that is one of the first teachers we should acknowledge and listen to, the great teacher that the body and the bones really are the bones of the warrioress."

16

THE FOUR DIRECTIONS OF WISE-BLOOD

I was deep in thought as I walked down the path from Agnes's cabin toward Dead Man's Creek. The clean, pine-scented air and the absence of sound made me think about my life and how I had come to work with these powerful women. I have always felt a longing for wholeness, for truth, for a sense of completeness. It is that yearning that placed my feet on the trail leading north to Agnes Whistling Elk and Ruby Plenty Chiefs so long ago. When I met these two extraordinary women of power, I saw my own reflection in their eyes. I saw how limited I was and how difficult it was going to be to move across the abyss from powerlessness to a place and position of power. But somewhere inside me was a need so great for unity, for that cocoon of universal love around me, that I went forward. I never asked; I never questioned; I never looked back. I simply moved down the empty path before me. On this path were citadels of encouragement, altars of prayer, and I made offerings along the way, offerings of parts of my collected baggage, pieces of myself that were no longer appropriate. It is a difficult journey, this pilgrimage toward enlightenment, so there had to be intent and will, strong and clear, to carry me along through the hard places.

• • •

I walked out of the forest into a meadow. The wild grass was green, lush, damp with morning dew. It reached above my knees, and I walked slowly, breathing deeply the aroma of fresh northern air. The scent of spring flowers was heady and relaxed me. I felt joyous. The thought of meeting with Woman at the Edge of Two Worlds had lifted my spirits greatly. I knew that I was passing through a gateway under a great elk skin, a symbol for the movement of a woman from one stage of life into another. This was not a quick passing. It was a long journey, one that had to be thoughtful and digested. I wanted to nourish that part of myself that was changing. I wanted to help myself feel comfortable. My consciousness was deep inside my own womb, and I felt the need for rest. I felt the need for peace, for a pulling together of the fragments of my life into one great shield of power and love.

As I walked through the meadow, I thought about the women that I had been working with, the women who were moving toward their own gateway, their own meeting with Woman at the Edge of Two Worlds. I considered what a powerful tradition for a changing woman this great goddess had given us. I thought about each of these women as if they were living in different directions, different aspects, on the sacred wheel. Each of them represented something different and special.

Beth, having gone into early menopause, is a woman who lives mostly in the south of the sacred wheel. She is an earth person, a physical person, a person who moves into the world as a storyteller. She knows the language of the stones, the bones of the earth. In the ceremony that we would be preparing for my four apprentice women, she would hold the power of the south direction, the power of trust and innocence, and the inner child. Her power animals are the ones with their noses closest to the ground. She has an ear to the surface of the earth like the mouse. She can hear far in the distance the vibration of movement, of danger. She has a great memory, and she has the ability to sit in the south and look to the north for spirit, spirit that can then be manifest into the physical world through her work with elderly people. She would one day be a great healer for people with bone diseases.

I moved down to the creek that meandered through the meadow. I sat by the banks of the smoothly flowing water for a long time and watched the reflections of the sky, the billowing clouds above, the sun sparkling on the water's surface like tumbling crystals. I watched the rainbow prisms that were created, and I felt the healing quality of the water current as it headed toward its destination—the sea, so very far away. I thought of Linda, whose husband had rejected her because she couldn't have more children, who would live in the west of the sacred wheel in the ceremony for her completion of her early life. Linda, a west woman, not unlike myself, lives in the sacred dream, constantly aware of the forces of nature, of death and rebirth, of transformation. She is a woman of the sacred dream. Her power animal is the great mother bear, the dreaming bear. She doesn't do too well in winter if much is asked of her. She wants to hibernate, move into her secret soul and experience the magic that she has stored there through the summer months. She likes to curl up with the things that she has learned and metabolize them and make them part of her own private dream. In her ability to control her emotions, which are vast, she then looks across the wheel to the east, to the process of mind and illumination, and she worships the rising sun that illuminates her spirit. I thought of her as I picked some flowers, yellow chamomile, that I would make into tea for her during the ceremony. I picked them carefully, choosing the ones that called to me for transformation. I placed them respectfully in a blue beaded pouch hanging from my belt.

I walked away from the stream, not really wanting to leave the edge of the water. I walked toward the mountains in the distance, the ground rising under my steps and lifting up toward the foothills. I looked at the snow-covered peaks and for a moment I felt the breeze that came off the tops of the mountains and

caressed my cheeks. I stood quietly in the stillness, not making a
sound. It was the kind of stillness into which all truth returns. I
welcomed the coolness that it brought, the gentleness. Then
came a gust of northerly wind, and the stern reminder of higher
realms of consciousness moved me on.

I walked toward an outcropping of rocks and climbed them as
if I were climbing the highest Himalayan mountain. I sat down
on the stones that had been warmed by the sun and placed my
hands on them, feeling their strength. The stones hold so many
memories, tell so many stories. I closed my eyes and thought of
Phyllis, who had always wanted to be a dancer, the north
woman, the woman of spirit, who had left her worldly life and
moved with wisdom into the Canadian tundra to live for a few
weeks in an isolated cabin to get to know herself again. She
chose to move into meditation, to live quietly, until her initiation
with us through the gateway with Woman at the Edge of Two
Worlds. She should be returning now, I thought, and she would
see the goddess very clearly. I smiled for a moment imagining her
excitement and her joy. She had great courage. She was very
good at choosing a target and aiming, pulling back the bow and
sending the arrow where it belonged. She was a brilliant woman.
Her education had served her well, but she had also learned in
the process of wisdom to let go of what worldly knowledge she
had gained and begin to move her consciousness into her body
mind and her shaman center around her navel. She felt her intent
every day and she meditated with nature. She had learned to
write about her experiences. I could see that she would be a fine
teacher in the world, that she had learned well. She had come
through our work together a bright beam of light. I thanked the
Great Spirit and Mother Earth for my meeting with her. She had
also taught me much.

I came down the outcropping of stone and moved off along
the east deer track toward a large meadow that stretched below,
golden, slightly tinged with green prairie grass and pink wildflowers. I sat at a vantage point and looked out across the vast

eastern plains. I had tears in my eyes as I thought of the great buffalo that had once roamed here and of the great purity of nature that had flourished untouched in its perfect splendor so long before we had come. I was deeply saddened for what we have done to so much of the wilderness of North America and to our planet's ecology. We have left so little of beauty for ourselves and our own children. Yet I remembered Agnes's words, that we choose to come here to learn, that the physical body is an extraordinary teacher and mirror for profound consciousness, if we only choose to see it. To heal Mother Earth, we must first heal ourselves.

I thought of Mary, who quite erroneously thought she was losing her beauty and sex appeal, my east apprentice. Her medicine is eagle. She flies highest and sees farthest. It is hard for Mary to relax into the consciousness of her body, to look across the sacred wheel at her emotions and feel, to allow herself to be vulnerable, because she is so stubbornly mental. This shamanistic teaching is not easy for Mary, but she is learning well and she will hold the power of the sacred circle in the east and never disown that power. When Mary had first come to me I remembered how she had denied the feelings that she was having about this passage in life. How strongly she had denied that anything was going on physically with her, until one day I began to see the beads of perspiration on her upper lip and forehead on a very cool afternoon, something that she could not mask, even though she was adept at wearing many personas in her life. Her favorite was, "I'm really only thirty-two, you know." The difference between her and so many people is that when she puts on a mask, she does it deliberately, and she also removes it when it is no longer needed. She realizes down deep that life is a great play, an intricate weaving of wills, a play of experience and evolvement. She knows that if for one moment she takes it all too seriously that depression will sweep over her and she will lose her way. She knows not to do that now.

Then I thought of myself as I sat still, looking out across the eastern plains. Strange dark clouds with an edge of gold sunlight were gathering in the distance. They would bring much needed rain. I could smell the dampness in the air. I moved down again into the meadow of this sacred circle. I could feel the presence of Agnes near me. I turned and saw Agnes walking out of a stand of aspen trees. She walked toward me, smiling. She was wearing a brightly colored woven skirt from Guatemala and a jean jacket over a yellow shirt. Her beaded shield hung around her neck and shone brightly with little facets gleaming reddish-brown and gold in the sunlight, like her eyes. I sat down in the meadow and made a place for her to sit with me. She joined me and touched my shoulder gently with the back of her hand and made a motion in sign language for heart and friendship. I looked at her and she looked into my eyes with a playful sense of humor.

"You're thinking about yourself again."

I laughed. "Yes, Agnes, I'm sitting in the center, in my mind, of my own sacred wheel. I was thinking about my apprentices and how we are such truthful mirrors for each other."

"Yes, my daughter, now you are beginning to learn. You were a great reflection for me and you still are."

"And how is that, Agnes?"

"You teach me how far I have come."

We both laughed. She slapped her knees and threw her head back as she so often had. Her mannerisms always warmed my heart and made me smile.

"I feel, Agnes, that I have a different path ahead, that there are many forks and many turnings in this new trail."

"Why do you see that?" Agnes asked.

"I'm not sure, but I see that part of this initiation of going through the sacred gateway of wise-blood with Woman at the Edge of Two Worlds is that I am moving into another level or round of life. In this process I look back over my life and I see that I must own what I have become."

"Are you not proud?" Agnes asked, taking a blade of new spring prairie grass and chewing on the tender, slightly yellow end. She waved the feathery tip of the grass at me like a tiny flag, toying with me ever so slightly with her eyes.

"I know in owning what I have become that I am very proud, Agnes Whistling Elk. You have taught me well, and I do not feel that you will ever cease to teach me, but I do see that there is a shift inside myself. I am becoming ever more the teacher, and oftentimes when I need you so, when I need to hear your voice, the sound of you comes up within me, almost as much as I hear you in the physical."

"Much of what you see today," Agnes said, "was helped by the grief of your mother's death. The grief so tremendously painful at the time deepened you in a way that helps you understand that there is no death, and in a sense there is no birth. We are a great circle."

I nodded in agreement and placed my palms down onto the earth, feeling the moisture coming up through the grasses. "I feel the earth, Agnes, truly as if she is my mother. I feel her gentle support and I know that she cries for help and understanding. I know that no one owns the truth, that we are all of one truth and one consciousness and that we are of the light. I feel so very full of love for you and for those that I work with. I want so much to help these women build their sacred lodges."

"Ah," Agnes said, sitting back for a moment, pinning me with her piercing gaze. I looked at her for several minutes, and then she added, "Those women that you teach are good women," she said, touching her heart with her fist, "but you must allow them to build their own lodges. You must allow them to stand alone."

I nodded, taking a deep breath, acknowledging what she was saying. "I try very hard, Agnes, to bring people to that woman of power within themselves. I try not to divide, to judge, to think for a moment that these women are healed because of me, for they have truly healed themselves."

"Ho," Agnes exclaimed with a smile. "Let them build their own lodges, Lynn. It would be wonderful if you could do it for them, but you cannot. Never forget my words. Come," she said.

"I think we need more silver sage from over there in the western part of the meadow. Do you remember your journey with Grandmother in England? Do you remember how she taught you to gather herbs?"

"Yes, Agnes, I do."

"Then come. We will enjoy ourselves."

I followed my sacred woman, my teacher, across the meadow toward the patch of silver-blue leaves of sage, and I felt the west wind come up and caress my face. It felt like a billowing silk scarf on a current of air. I was full in my heart.

17

OLD MAMA SQUIRREL AND THE HERBS FOR MENOPAUSE

The next morning I sat with Ruby, tying bundles of sage. "Many women living through different stages of life and development are fascinated with looking forward into what is about to happen to them in a physiological sense," I said. "For instance, young girls are very interested in what the passage of giving birth entails. They are full of wonderment about their own ability to give life. Women in their thirties, I find, are also very fascinated with the process of menopause."

We were sitting on the porch of Ruby's cabin. Ruby, her long hair pulled back and braided, was whittling on a stick with her buck knife and turning her head from side to side with the cadence of my words. Finally, she stomped her booted foot and said, "Yah, yah, yah, yah." And I looked at her, stopping my thoughts, wondering what was the matter with her. Ruby said nothing more.

"Ruby, what's the matter?" I finally asked.

"A lot of words," she said. "Words, a lot of words."

"Well, would you rather I stopped talking?" I asked her.

"No, but I'd like you to rethink what you're saying," she said. "You just sound boring, that's all," Ruby sniffed, taking a swipe with her knife. A chip of willow branch flipped off onto the old worn boards of the porch.

"Well, thank you very much," I said. "I'm just trying to tell you—"

Ruby interrupted me again. "You sound just like a teacher. You sound like someone sitting in a schoolroom, a schoolroom that is painted pukey green with a bunch of bored people sitting in little oak chairs, upright and uncomfortable." She brushed wood chips off her faded jean skirt and shirt.

I had to laugh at the memory of sitting in just such a room as a young girl in Seattle, Washington.

"Don't you remember anything, Lynn?"

"Anything about what?" I asked.

"Anything about what we've taught you."

"I think I've remembered a lot."

"Remember," Ruby said, picking up the stick and pointing it at me menacingly, "you never learn through hearing borrowed knowledge. It may sound good; it may even be intelligent, but when you speak to people about something that is not part of their own dream, part of their own experience, they can never own what you say. They can never make it part of their own world."

I looked out across the clearing and into the trees. The poplar leaves were quaking in the afternoon breeze, catching the light like tiny shards of mirror reflecting brilliant beams of gold into the forest. I took a deep breath and sat back against the wall of the porch and nodded my head.

"Ruby, you're right. Thank you for reminding me."

Ruby went on whittling and finally held up a tiny figure of a wolf howling at the moon. She held it out to me. "See, one of your power animals is black wolf. Here she is howling at the moon. You are not truly a wolf, but there is part of your spirit that is a wolf, just like in every woman there is a part of the spirit that has already been old, that has already been the old wise one, the holder of wise-blood, the old one who knows many ways, who picks up the trail. Even if you're thirteen years old or twenty years old, there's a part of you that knows what that's like. When you hold that tiny wolf in your hand, there's a part of your spirit that knows what it's like to howl at the moon. Is that not so?" She wrinkled her nose at me and smiled.

"This is true, Ruby. I have always felt that I know."

"And all women," Ruby said, "know that they know. From the moment they put their little feet down on this great Mother Earth, women *know* and are familiar with her energy because it is female."

"So what are you saying, Ruby?"

"I am telling you to give your people the experience of initiation. Give them the experience of what it is like to move from one level of consciousness to another."

"But how can I do that, Ruby? I cannot take a twenty-year-old girl through the gateway of menopause."

"No, but you can teach her the old way. You can teach her to serve the old wise ones around her." She winked at me. "There are certain ceremonies that younger women cannot be present at, but they can be present at the celebration. They can certainly listen to the women who have gone through the gateway. Meanwhile, when you speak to your women of emotions, of hormones, and so forth, always bring them through a visualization process, so that everything becomes real to them. Your words become more than simply sound. Those sounds can take form in their mind's eye, and that form begins to dance in the world of their reality."

"I have been struggling for months with the concept of initiation around the process of menopause," I said. "I cannot reveal all of the secrets of the Sisterhood in that event."

"No," Ruby said, "you cannot, but you can impart the feeling of celebration. You can impart many of the ceremonies that we are teaching you. You understand what I mean, because Woman at the Edge of Two Worlds will have become part of your council fires. It is also time for her to be introduced to your realm of existence in twentieth-century life. Counsel with her and us. We will guide you on your path."

Just then I heard a rustling in the bushes to the right of the cabin. "*Namaste,*" I heard a familiar voice say in welcome. I turned to see the bright face of July, Ruby's young apprentice. I had not seen her in over a year. I rushed down the steps of the porch to give her a big hug. July was so beautiful.

"Your hair is lovely, July," I said, stroking the long black hair that hung to her waist. Her face was full of light and happiness.

"Oh, Lynn, my heart is full. I have not seen you in such a long time. We have lots to share." She indicated many bags that she held in her hands and over one shoulder. "Come, let's go to my favorite clearing in the forest. I have much to show you."

"But July, I didn't even know you were coming."

We walked up onto the porch and July handed one of the bags to Ruby. Ruby smiled, opening the bag. She took a long, deep breath, inhaling the scent of its contents.

"Ah," she said. "You two run off." She spoke as if she were speaking to young children. "I am going to prepare an ointment from these herbs," she said to July. "Thank you, my daughter." She bowed slightly from the waist and went into her cabin.

"Come," July said. "Ruby and I have been preparing something. I have much to tell you. This will be fun."

We walked down the path hand in hand. The west wind had come up, bringing the scent of the plains and pine, as we walked through the poplar trees. I noticed that they were looking strong and healthy in the spring light. Finally, we came to a clearing that was hollowed out under the poplar trees, the branches above us cathedrallike, shading us from the intense sunlight. We sat down on two flat rocks, another flat piece of sandstone between us. July brushed off the sandstone with her hands and laid five small pouches around the rock.

"Ruby has asked me to gather many herbs for you. They are teaching herbs. They are herbs that the two of us gathered at proper phases of the moon. We gathered them in a sacred way and they are for you."

"What herbs are they?" I asked, tremendously excited.

"These herbs are used by our ancient sisters and by all of the women in the Sisterhood. A few of these plants are almost extinct. I want to lay herbs out next to each other so that you can see what they look like and the differences among them. There is one in particular that is very important for women going through this Changing Woman transition," July said, "and Ruby asked me to show her to you first."

I remembered back to what Ruby had said about the younger woman serving the older woman. I sat back and allowed July to prepare her bags, which seemed very precious to her. First she opened a rawhide pouch and very carefully extracted ten or twenty leaves.

"We call this plant 'leaves of light,'" she said and then mentioned a Native American word that I had not heard before, meaning leaves of light. "See how smooth they are." She handed me a leaf. It felt smooth on one side, almost glasslike in its smoothness. "These leaves of light are like or have a similar effect to the black cohash root that you find in your health food stores. This is a very important plant for times of transition and hormonal imbalance."

Very carefully and with great reverence, July took leaves from the other pouches and placed them around the circle. "This black cohash root is sometimes called rattle root or squaw root and lives in the south," she said. "They are for the physical body and for giving you more trust in the process that is happening to you during hormonal imbalance. It also lowers blood pressure and cholesterol levels, relieves hot flashes and menstrual cramps."

From the next pouch she took out some berries, little pinkish-red berries, some tinged with green, and she placed these in the west. She said, "These are not unlike your belladonna or dong quai from China. They have a calming effect on you, one that calms the emotions, so it is called a west plant. It is a plant that has to be carefully harvested during the full moon. It is a plant that you must carefully take—not the elders, the strongest ones, because they are needed to create new herbs for the following year, and also not the young ones. You take the middle ones and that is what is gathered here. These can be dried and ground into a fine powder to be added to the leaves of light and they balance very well."

Then she reached into another pouch, a very soft deerskin pouch, and gently she brought out four or five twigs. She placed these in the east. "These are twigs from a certain kind of elm. They are like your slippery elm in that they help you to balance your retention of water, the water weight that comes with hormonal imbalance, and help to ease PMS," July said. "Slippery elm has calcium, vitamins A and B, and phosphorus, all of which are good for bone formation."

I could tell that she was trying to remember the facts that she had learned about these plants. Her face was so beautiful and so serene. Patterns of light from the branches filtering the sunlight above played across her cheeks as she spoke. Her eyes flashed with excitement. Her long red skirt and white blouse accentuated the deeply tanned color of her skin. Her silver and turquoise bracelet occasionally exploded in a bright silvery reflection of sun as she worked with her plants and carefully fashioned her teaching for me.

Next she took out buds that looked like thistles, lavender and prickly, and placed them in the north. "These," she said, "are sacred thistles." She pronounced a Native American name for them. "These are blessed thistles that you are familiar with from your health food stores. This blessed thistle when mixed with these other herbs makes a very fine combination. It relieves PMS, increases circulation, and strengthens the heart. It's also good for the brain, which we can all use," she laughed.

Then she took out another bag filled with roots and branches and leaves, a much larger bag, and she set them in the center.

"This is an almost extinct plant. For some reason it is known to my people as the 'virgin tree.' It is very similar and has the estrogen content that dong quai has. Dong quai, as you know, Lynn, is the herb that comes from China and is extremely helpful with women having estrogen problems. It helps with hot flashes, carries vitamins A, B^{12}, and E, aids in preventing vaginal dryness, and increases the function of ovarian hormones. This plant"— she pointed to a pile of small leaves—"contains estrogen, and it is simple clover. If horses eat it, because of the high estrogen it gives them laminitis in their hooves."

I recognized how carefully chosen July's words were. I reached across and touched her hand, looking into her eyes. "You have worked very hard to present this knowledge to me, and I appreciate it, July. Thank you."

She smiled at me and blushed gently. "So, Lynn, to be complete, combine a mixture of black cohash root, blessed thistle herb, squaw vine herb, sasparilla root, Siberian ginseng root, like this." She cupped her hand, showing the hollow of her palm fitted with powdered leaves and roots. She pointed to a small, whitish root. "I included that. I didn't dig it up here. And that's the sasparilla, which also came from the West, as did the licorice root, which is right here." She touched the dark root gently with her fingers. "Here is the false unicorn root that Grandmother Twin Dreamers gave me. She said it is excellent for all menopausal symptoms, and it tones the uterus. So all of these herbs can be ground together in equal portions and taken in capsules or a tea form." She then handed me a full cotton bag with a draw string.

"What's this?" I asked.

"This is your first bag of Changing Woman herbs to make you feel ever so good," July said proudly and with a big smile. "You don't have to do this, but there are more of the first herbs and roots that I mentioned, getting proportionately less by a pinch or so as I went down the list. That's my formula. This is also an excellent combination for PMS and mood swings. It really mellows you out."

"July, thank you so much. I'll try some the moment we get back to the cabin."

As she set the bags down, a quick movement off to my left caught my eye. Before we could say another word, a squirrel had suddenly jumped into our circle. She sat at the edge of the rock on her hind legs, holding her little paws in front of her, looking as if she were going to try to steal some of the leaves. July and I looked at each other in surprise, saying nothing. Neither of us knew quite what to do. As I looked at the squirrel I could tell that she was very old. She had grey fur around the ruff of her neck. I was taken aback and wondered what in the world was happening here. Then the squirrel, snapping her tail from side to side, started chattering away. She looked at me and chattered and chattered as if she were scolding madly. Switching her tail back and forth, she ran in little circles around and around. Then she jumped up onto one of the bags. For a moment I thought July was going to prevent her, but July sat back also in wonderment at the behavior of this squirrel. Then, very gently, the old mama squirrel took the leaves of light and held one as if holding it up to the sunlight, and then ran around again and put the leaf down.

July said, "Oh, I almost forgot. When you pick the leaves of light, you must hold the leaves up to the sun. You must hold them up to the sun to see the density. See the veins?" She pointed. "Those veins will tell you whether this is the right leaf or not."

"You mean those little indentations there," I said, pointing with my finger.

"Yes," July said, "If they have turned red, they are not to be picked."

My eyes opened wide, and I looked down at the squirrel who was sitting in the middle of the stone, calmly eating one of the leaves of light. She switched her tail, chattered some more at me, and then from each of the four directions, she took a sample and another nibble, looking at the leaves as she did so. Even the thistle, she held up very gently in her paws, sniffed at it, and chattered away at both July and me while switching her tail. When she got to the twigs that were sitting in the east, she started peeling off the bark of one of the twigs.

"Oh," July said, "I forgot again. You have to peel off the bark of the twigs, and it's what's inside the bark that is so valuable. It has a natural progesterone in it, and that progesterone is what you need to balance the estrogen so that you will not be out of balance and the disease of cancer is not given strength."

"I don't understand," I said.

"What I mean is that estrogen so often needs to be balanced with progesterone so that the endometrial lining of the uterus does not build up. Progesterone makes you cycle."

As she said this the squirrel ran in little circles, chattering and scolding both of us as if we were truant school children. I sat back, wondering if I was really seeing a squirrel doing this. And at exactly the same moment July and I had a similar thought. Both of us looked down at the mama squirrel to see if there was anything in that squirrel that might remind us of Ruby. As we did this, the squirrel, with a flick of her tail, ran off the stone, out into the meadow, and disappeared. She had left quite a mess of pieces of leaves and sticks and roots strewn everywhere. Everything was in disarray.

"You know, July, this reminds me of something," and I had to laugh. "I don't know if that was just a squirrel looking for a free lunch or what, but I remember when we were in Australia, working with Ginevee and the aboriginal women in the outback. Remember when I was writing *Crystal Woman*?" July nodded. "I was making a sand painting called a *pupunya*, and I had worked for days and days gathering the sand and making sure that the colors were correct. I had begun my sand painting and it had taken me all through four nights and days to design. I sat in my little wurly against the wind so that my sand painting would not be disrupted, and suddenly from out of nowhere in the early morning came Ruby, walking in bare feet. She walked right through the center of my sand painting, casting my dreams and my hopes to the four winds. I will never forget it. She wanted to know why I had not represented the great unknown out of which the mysteries of power are born."

"Yes, I remember, I remember," July said.

"Well, July, does this not feel a bit reminiscent of that?"

July was wide eyed as if she couldn't quite believe what her mind was beginning to think.

"Partly, the wondrousness of the teachings of the Sisterhood of the Shields is that so many mysterious events occur, and all I can say, July, is that we can take each other to the point of knowing; we can take each other to the place of the great mystery, to the edge of the abyss, but beyond that point there is no explanation. I cannot tell you why these things happen. I cannot tell you why someone has power and another does not. I can help you get to the place of power, but it is your choice to take that power."

"Yes, yes," July said, clapping her hands, "and that's what these plants do."

"Yes, they do, don't they? They can help your body to adjust to the nature of your own rhythms and of life, but you have to add another ingredient. As Ruby said so well when she walked through my sand painting in Australia, 'Where is the unknowable? Where is the unknowable represented?' And I had said, 'But nowhere.' And she said, 'Then your sand painting has no power, because power is born from the unknowable, from that place that cannot be explained, that place of bliss, of perfection, that place where the Great Spirit lives within you. It is to that place that initiation can take you.'"

"Yes," July said, "and I hope that I will be able to do that one day."

"July, one day you, too, will walk through the gateway of Woman at the Edge of Two Worlds, as all women will walk through that gateway. But the true initiation comes from your effort, your desire to be whole. Initiation, knowledge, wisdom can be presented to someone, but if they cannot hear it, it does them no good."

"That is why you put people through an experience," July said, her hair beginning to sway in the breeze as she turned her head this way and that.

"Yes, July, that is correct. We must experience what we learn so that it becomes true. We must eat of that knowledge, just like that squirrel. She came up here and she ate of all of the leaves and twigs. It is just like an idea that is placed on the sacred wheel. If we do not eat of what we learn, then it means nothing to us."

"Ah," July said, "does that mean that when you go through the gateway with Woman at the Edge of Two Worlds that you actually eat something?"

"Yes, I believe you do. You eat of an offering. It's a giveaway, a symbol for the transformational process. When you eat the leaves of a plant, that plant is transformed by you into something quite different from what it was. You help it to move on to a higher level. That is something also in Australia that I had great difficulty with. I learned that from Ginevee more than anyone else. So maybe that little squirrel, whoever that little squirrel was—she was an old girl, an elderly soul—maybe she knows. Even the squirrel world may know that these plants help. Even the animals go through periods of transition. Maybe to her these plants were something that she craved, and we had gathered them all together just for her."

July and I picked up the leaves and twigs and put them in their proper pouches. I gave July a big hug and took off the coral ring I wore on my right hand and gave it to her in gratitude for her work with me. We sat for a long time in the poplar forest, laughing and talking about what had been happening. We were really waiting for old mama squirrel to return, but she did not.

THE CAULDRON OF TRUTH

AFTER YOU HAVE REALIZED

MENOPAUSE

"You are woman. You are like fire now—you reach for the wise goddess mother in the sky," Woman at the Edge of Two Worlds said to me. "She comes to you. She is you. Remember always who you are."

18

THE LODGE OF THE WANING MOON

That night we sat in ceremony with the rest of the women from the Sisterhood, who had arrived during the day. We sat smoking the sacred pipe of the Sisterhood of the Shields, saying prayers for different aspects of the healing of Mother Earth. We had all come together for the first time in a very long while, and we spent several days getting reacquainted and talking about our families, our apprentices, and the work that we had been doing. It was clear to me that we were gathered together during the waning moon, especially this year, for a ceremony to meet the great goddess figure, Woman at the Edge of Two Worlds. She is the goddess that I had heard about since I was initiated into the Sisterhood of the Shields. As Agnes had explained to me, she was the great goddess for all changing women moving through the gateway of menopause.

To my great surprise and excitement, Zoila's apprentice, Olivia, from Solola, Guatemala, was moving through the same gateway as I. We would be doing this ceremony together. It was the first time in my history with the Sisterhood of the Shields that I would be sharing a ceremony with another woman who was also being initiated as I was. Always before I was the only one moving through a passage or a gateway. I was excited to have another woman to converse with who was going through a similar experience. Olivia was about five foot three. She looked warm and kind. Her body was round and stocky, and she moved with a surprising power and grace for someone built so close to the ground. She had long, sleek black hair touched with gray that she normally wore in braids. She wore the traditional woven *huipile* and jean-type skirt with patches of brightly colored weaving sewn together. She usually went barefoot or wore leather sandals, and her demeanor was normally placid, serene, and reflective, like the magnificent shaman lake, Lake Atitlan, around which she had spent all of her life.

I remembered Lake Atitlan, the lake at the foot of the volcanos. When I had first worked with Zoila and Jose in Guatemala and Yucatan, while I was writing my book *Jaguar Woman,* I would sit by the lake for hours and watch my reflection and the reflection of the clouds overhead. I would sit there until nightfall when I could look up at the cliffs coming down from Solola into Panahachel. Occasionally a tourist bus or truck would wind its way back up to the plateau leading into Antigua. But I was there to watch the shaman fires lit in the caves above the lake. At that time I was not allowed into those ceremonies. It wasn't until much later in my work with Agnes and Ruby that I was invited there into the transformational caves of healing and power. As I sat by the lake, I felt as if the stars had fallen from the heavens and landed and set themselves sparkling and bright into the walls of the cliffs above me. I had been told by Zoila never to swim in the lake after four o'clock, because every so often the volcano would adjust itself and a small tidal wave would swell up in the lake and drown anybody on it. It was a very treacherous body of water, full of mystery and deep intrigue down into its murky depths.

As I watched Olivia, I could see Lake Atitlan reflected in her behavior. This was not a woman to be played with. I could see her heritage in every movement of her body, the heritage of ancient Mayan culture that had been all but destroyed by the

Western civilization. Fortunately, in Guatemala the native people were allowed to live in their villages and worship their own gods and goddesses right alongside the Catholic deities. But I could see the hiddenness, the quality of secretiveness, in Olivia because of the way she had been raised. It was not allowed for shamans to gather more than a few people together at a time for a healing. It was punishable by death if more than a hundred people gathered at the great sacred altars of stone, "the faces of the earth," upon which shamans placed their sacred bundles and prayers. I watched this woman from a distance at first, not having met her. I wanted to know her first in a more subtle way.

One morning I had been sitting on Ruby's porch, talking with her about squaw vine and other herbs that we had found the day before. Out of the clearing came Zoila dressed in a white cotton peasant blouse, a cotton shawl woven in yellow and red, a woven skirt from Guatemala, and sandals. Next to her walked Olivia, dressed in the thin white cotton of the Yucatan, embroidered with figures here and there. Her long black hair was tied back. Her face shone with a youthful quality of innocence and also formidable power, if one were to look closely into her eyes. She looked thirty, I thought, except for the few strands of gray hair around the crown of her head. She walked over to me with strong strides. She and Zoila had brought a basket of fruit. They laid it down on the porch and knelt down on the steps, smiling. Zoila introduced us.

"Lynn, my daughter, one who has worked for so long with all of us, one who is close to my heart, I want you to meet and honor my apprentice, my daughter Olivia."

I had been waiting for them. Sitting before Olivia I gave her the beaded hair ties that I had been saving for her. We hugged each other. Olivia spoke broken English as I struggled with Quiche and Spanish, but it didn't seem to matter. It was very clear that we understood each other without words.

Ruby came over and sat with us on the edge of the porch. She took the basket of fruit and held an apple up to the sun. "Let the sun give you power," she said, holding up the apple to the sun and petting it as if it were a young pup. She took a big bite of the apple, smacking her lips and chewing voraciously with great pleasure. She offered the apple to me. I took a bite and then offered it to Olivia. We became instant friends.

I remembered when I met the sacred clan in Australia with Ginevee and how we had all stripped naked, as was their custom, and held each other and became, not sexual, but close, understanding each other's physical bodies as well as each other's spirits. I held Olivia's hands in mine. I stroked her fingers and looked at the palms of her hands. The pads of her hands were heavy and thick from hard work, callused like a man's. I smiled. She smiled back at me as she looked at my hands, seeing how different they were. She felt the calluses on the fingers of my writing hand. We laughed at the differences between us. She pinched my shoulder, and I pinched a tiny roll of flesh above the waistband on her skirt. We laughed and our teachers laughed with us.

Zoila stood. "Today, my daughters, you will be entering the moon lodge."

"The moon lodge?" I said.

"Yes, the waning moon lodge. It is different from any lodge that you have entered before. It is a willow lodge out in the trees. Tonight you and Olivia will spend the evening. You will do a cleansing sweat together and you will share your spirits. You will talk of your experiences and your fears, of what it is like to be moving through this initiation. You will share whatever is in your heart to share. I would like you to prepare now. You have fasted for two days. Take your sacred things, Lynn. Take your drum and what is needed for you to pray and be comfortable. Bring your blanket. We will meet you down by the creek when the sun is moving toward the horizon.

An hour later Agnes and Ruby and I were walking down toward Dead Man's Creek. I saw a bent willow lodge nestled into the poplar trees. It was not far from the banks of the water that meandered slowly and happily in the setting sun, reflecting orange and purple prisms of light into the northern air. We entered the sweat lodge by the creek and prayed with our teachers until the moon was high. Then we all followed Agnes up the trail. The waning moon lodge was not unlike my Dreamlodge, made out of bent willows, covered with sacred blankets of every color, reds and blues and blacks and grays. There were Navajo blankets and blankets from South America, from Peru and Ecuador. There were blankets from Nepal and Tibet, blankets from North America and Europe, blankets that represented the women who were gathered here from around the earth to honor us and help us through our passage.

Together Olivia and I parted two blankets that hung over the doorway. One of the blankets was from Guatemala and the other was from Two Grey Hills in the Southwest. I sensed that one blanket represented the continent from which I had received my teaching and the other blanket represented Olivia's country. Inside was a fire smoldering in the center, its coals shining like cat's eyes in the interior darkness of the lodge. Sacred baskets with the symbols for woman, corn, and rain woven into them, drums, blankets, bundles of dried sweetgrass, sprigs of cedar and juniper, several beaded bags, and various herbs tied with red yarn hung from the rafters of the lodge. There were two gourds in front of the fire, specially placed. Every stone was set carefully, one against the other, each representing prayers from the women for our journey.

I sat in the west direction around the fire, holding my position of power that I had learned so well. Facing me in the east was Olivia, so obviously an east woman, a woman of vision, a woman who danced her power into the world, a woman who was also mysterious. A great deal of her power and knowledge was hidden so that she could survive in a country that did not allow women to be powerful except at prescribed times. Agnes and Ruby used their mother rattles and celestial rattles, and, shaking them in a swish of sound like water over a fall, they said prayers and we prayed with them. Then we chanted. Soon Agnes, Ruby, and Zoila left us, leaving the moon lodge through the blanketed entrance.

I picked up the gourds, each about ten inches in diameter, that had been placed before us in our circle. I handed one to Olivia. Each had been cut about three-quarters of the way up so that there was a top. I removed it. The gourds had been smudged and blessed.

"These gourds are like the Marriage Basket," Agnes had told us. "The gourd represents your womb. Place your prayers and the magic of your spirit within it. Later you will paint it and awaken the guardians who protect it."

We blessed them with sage and sweetgrass and fresh cedar that had been newly dried for this ceremony. I asked the Great Spirit and Mother Earth to hear me, to listen to my prayers, and to help me on my journey. I called in my power animals. I called for guidance and understanding from all of my ancestors and those who love me.

Olivia lit candles around the fire. The lodge was very dark inside, and we could see the waning moon above us through the smoke hole and the midnight blue sky. We took our gourds and held them up to the sky fathers and down to Mother Earth, and all mystery faded from our expressions, as if a curtain had been pulled away. We set the gourds in our laps as we spoke.

In front of us were two pots of red clay placed there by Ruby. She had said, "The teachings of Woman at the Edge of Two Worlds are of the words and blood of Mother Earth. So take this red clay as you speak your truth to each other, take a little spring water out of this water basket, and make a symbol with clay and your fingers for each idea that you tell. It is simple, it is the old way, and in the beginning it is how the children were made. Place each figure into your gourd womb. They will hold your female life force. Later we will set them in the male shine of the sun to be made strong, because truth is always about balance of energy even in the ceremonies of the waning moon."

Olivia's face became suddenly vulnerable and open with no reservation, no qualification to her words. Even her voice shifted and changed as she began to speak entirely from her heart. "I thank you, my sister, for being with me at this time," Olivia said. "It has been hard for me, because I know I can no longer have children, and that is important in my culture—to be fertile, to give boy children life to harvest the fields to become strong so that we may live." Olivia created a small clay figure with her fingers as she spoke. "I no longer can have more daughters to help me to weave, to gather the corn, to make clothes to sell in the marketplace in Chichicastanengo. I am frightened, sister. My uterus was taken surgically. I had a benign tumor. So this time of wise-blood has come upon me so suddenly that I have not been able to prepare myself in my mind or in my heart."

Correspondingly, I felt the persona of strength and power fading away from my own face. I felt comfortable in my own vulnerability, in my own honesty and clarity. "I feel anxious, my sister," I said, "not because of a loss of fertility, but because I know that there is not much time left, and I pray that I will have the means to continue my work." I reached into the damp clay, and taking a small amount, I began to work with it. "I pray that even along the wisdom path in this aging process that I, as a grandmother, will still be listened to. My culture tends not to recognize their grandmothers. I hope that people that I work with who read my words will understand that in the elders is held the wisdom. In my society, in my world, the elders are not respected as they should be, Olivia. Youth is truth in my world."

Olivia nodded. That was partly true of her world as well. I offered cornmeal to the Great Mother and placed it into my gourd bowl along with a tiny clay figure. I took some more clay, as did Olivia.

"I fear that this work, which is so important and could heal the earth with its female consciousness, may not be given as much credence if I am a grandmother, if my beauty changes," I said hesitatingly, realizing for the first time that I really felt this fear.

Olivia laughed with my last words and nodded her head and said, "Yes, sister, I understand. My husband is already looking at younger women."

"Isn't it interesting," I said, "because it is now in these middle years that men and women need each other so much. It is now that partnership really becomes a deep friendship, because we do need help and support. We need to give assistance. We need that kind of love and caring that comes with long relationships, relationships that have been tried through time and found to be strong. Still, we fear for our lack of sexuality. The men fear for their virility; the women fear for their fertility and attractiveness. Actually, it is such a relief, in a way, to be able to live differently at long last."

Olivia laughed, not unlike Agnes, slapping her thighs, very open in her throat and voice as we talked into the night. No power held in her throat, I thought, as I smiled back at her, enjoying our communion.

"You know, sister," Olivia said, "as I speak to you, I begin to see that perhaps it is not so important, my fears."

I agreed with her. "It's true. In my country people spend fortunes on therapy, because the stress is so enormous."

"Yes," Olivia said, "how do you live in cars and buildings that are high above the ground, so far from Mother Earth, everything covered in concrete? How do you live without the feel of Mother Earth under your bare feet?"

"Oh, it is very difficult, Olivia. When I come back from working with my women in the wilderness of Canada or Tibet or wherever we are, I always feel like a cocoon of synthetic material has been dropped around my body as I enter the city. It's as if I lose part of my freedom."

She cocked her head, not fully understanding the word *synthetic*.

"When I say *synthetic*," I said, "what I mean is that we are so separated from what is real, from what is natural. It is, unfortunately, the natural thing for us to breathe air that has been recycled through air conditioning systems on our airplanes and in our buildings that are closed without windows that open. We wear clothing next to our skin that is not of the earth. It is not natural silk or wool or cotton, but synthesized, created by man because of the shortage of materials, or so that it is less expensive to create. There are so many people in the world, Olivia," I said, putting another pinch of cornmeal and another clay figure into my gourd.

"Yes, my sister," she said with a sweeping movement of her arms. "Perhaps it is better for me not to have more children," she laughed. "I have had already seven children, four boys and three girls, but we all work the land and weave to support our family."

"That's a big family," I said. "I have only one daughter, and she is so dear to me." I offered sage smoke, a prayer, and another figure for my daughter that she be strong and find her way with joy and happiness in the world.

"Olivia, you have been raised so differently from me. You have been raised mostly in nature, in a village with your whole family surrounding you, almost a tribal situation. You have been raised with sacredness. You have been raised with your traditions. You have also lived with tremendous fear that it would all be taken away from you, but you have done so well, my sister. I can see that you have learned well, that your power is intact. I have lived a different life from you in the cities of the world. Fortunately, in my early life I lived on a small farm in eastern Washington state. We had horses and animals, and even though my family was tremendously disrupted and I had no brothers and sisters and I was very lonely, I had my Native American friends from the Spokane area who gave me such strength in those days when I was so young. Even though I live in the cities now, I do not forget the earth. I do not forget what it feels like to have the north wind in my hair. When I ache to go back to the high sounds of the wind in the pine trees, I know that I can find Agnes and Ruby in the Dreamtime, if they are not physically nearby. I can relive that experience of heart and be brought back to my center.

"I look across the sacred fire at you, my sister, and I realize that we are not that different. We, as women, share a common understanding of what is real and what is true for the nurturing of life, however that is done, for the nurturing of our own soul. I feel that we have a responsibility, Olivia, to live in a way that will strengthen our spirit in our life, so that if the world goes into more depression ecologically and economically, we will still be alive to teach. That is our responsibility, and that is why we work together to preserve the sacred and ancient way of woman. I see that we are of one spirit, that in a sense you and I need not even speak, because there is deep understanding in your eyes and I feel your love, Olivia. I feel your pain, for it is mine as well. I also realize that I cannot carry your grief, as you cannot carry mine."

After putting another pinch of cornmeal in my gourd, I lit some copal and herbal incense. Taking a long breath of the special blend of herbs, I blew my breath to the four directions and asked for guidance from the Great Spirit who lives within us. Then I offered my gourd and the smoke to Mother Earth. Olivia held her gourd bowl in her left hand and one of her many clay figures in her right hand. She held them up to the moon and chanted and prayed in Quiche with tears streaming down her cheeks. I played my drum which had been given to me and awakened by Agnes Whistling Elk. It is my personal drum, and with it I had been taught how to pray and sing with the Sisterhood of the Shields in their way. I could see that Olivia could feel the love and the power that lived within my drum. She joined me in a chant taught to us by the Sisterhood. It was about the sacred power of woman. Olivia and I, with our eyes closed, swung clockwise in a dance around the fire, honoring the four directions. Then, holding the bowls respectfully to our hearts and a figure to the moon, we sang asking for blessings and understanding. Relighting the sage and sweetgrass, we blessed our gourds filled with red clay symbols and the words from our hearts. It is our tradition that over the sacred fire only truth may be spoken.

Late into the night we talked of our children and our hearts until happy and exhausted. We talked with anticipation and excitement about our initiations with Woman at the Edge of Two Worlds to come during the next night of ceremony. We both realized that this was our last night in our first ring of power. As we entered tomorrow into the gateway of Changing Woman, our lives would become a different reality forever. Finally, we curled up in our blankets and slept our first time in the lodge of the waning moon.

19

WOMAN AT THE EDGE OF TWO WORLDS

I sat in the center of a great circle, cedar smoke from the sacred fire drifting like a sleeping dragon around us. Each of the women from the Sisterhood of the Shields was represented. Our magnificent painted shields globes—some ancient in origin with splashes of lightning, symbols of thunder lords and goddesses of rain holding eagle feathers and beaded gourds—were displayed on tripods behind where we sat. We had been doing ceremony for many hours, playing our medicine drums, smoking our ceremonial pipe, and talking among ourselves from time to time. Occasionally, the aurora borealis, visible in this part of the far north of Canada, would streak the sky with pulsations of orange and pink, and sometimes a flash of gold.

There were forty-four of us, and we had paused for a moment to meditate and move silently into our place of power. From a stand of poplar trees off to the north, down toward Dead Man's Creek, came an extraordinary sound, a primal growl that turned into a deafening roar. I had never heard an animal sound quite like this. We all looked at each other and then toward the trees, as we saw a giant shadow moving out from the darkness. The shadow was a hulk, tall and shaped like a large man, moving toward us through the smokey haze. Then, as the fire flared, we could see that a giant female polar bear was standing on her hind legs, foaming at the mouth and roaring as if one of us had threatened her life.

The woman known as Jaguar Woman began to play her drum, and the others followed. I held my drum, but in my terror, I seemed unable to move. The drumming became louder, and the sound began to move in a directional way from south to west to north to east, spiraling into a vibrating dance of hypnotic sound. I could not understand why everyone continued to play their drums, while this gigantic silvery white ghost of a bear, obviously ferocious and angry, was entering our circle. I have always had grave respect and a sense of honor for the great dreaming bears of the west on the sacred wheel, but I also had tremendous respect for their ability to kill you with one swipe of a giant paw.

Her claws glistened in the firelight. Her teeth were bared, and foam dropped from her mouth onto her shiny white fur. She swayed in the moonlight as if in some mysterious way she had been touched by the sound of our magic, as if she was meant to be there within our circle and was answering the throbbing call of the beating heart within our medicine drums. She walked on her hind legs, clawing the sky with her forelegs, throwing her head this way and that. She turned completely around and dropped down onto four legs, tossing her head in what looked like a blind rage.

The Sisterhood continued to play the drums. The sound was a tympany of beats that meshed together into the most unbelievable fabric of primal music I think I have ever heard. The beat was extraordinary and each woman seemed to be playing in rhythm and in complement with the woman sitting next to her. The rhythm was very complicated and different from anything we usually played. Occasionally, my hand would caress my drum, and for a moment I would remember to play it. Then my consciousness would swirl in my head to the rhythm. I seemed to be moving between the subconscious dream and conscious reality. I think it was only the terror that kept me from passing out right there on the spot. I knew instinctively that I was not to get up and run, that somehow what was happening with this great shimmering white bear was meant to happen.

Now she stood up again on her hind legs, her fur thick and rippling in waves, and she moved around the circle, looking into the eyes of one sister after another. Some of the women would reach out to her, unafraid, as if this great bear, this roaring extraordinary creature were only a vision and not a vicious animal that could tear them asunder in a moment. The bear turned around again, almost twirling as the drumbeat accelerated into a frenzy. Then with a lurch, still maintaining her balance on her hind legs, she walked toward me. She pinned me with her ferocious gaze, her antique gold eyes reflecting the light from the flames. My terror was so profound that I could not run, though I wanted to. At that point I don't know if I stayed conscious or was gifted with a beautiful teaching dream. But nevertheless, I experienced the events that came next and that I will share with you.

Suddenly, with a gracefulness not of a bear but of a goddess, she reached down, and I felt her paws, huge claws, around my midsection. She lifted me into the air. I screamed, but no sound would come. I was rigid in panic and fright. I knew that this was medicine, that I was to understand what was happening, but my fright took over and I was as rigid as a prayer stick in her paws. She lifted me up as I had seen Agnes lift up her sacred pipe so often to the rising sun. She lifted me up to the waning moon and she turned me to the four directions.

Then I heard a voice. I did not know where it came from. It could have been the great bear. It did not matter. The voice was female, and it was strong and somehow comforting to me. I was still held by the great bear in the center of the fire circle, as if I were being presented to the gods for some kind of sacrifice or a rite of passage. The terror that had so filled me began to leave my body, like water pouring out of a cup. And then she said to me, "In this sacred dream that we call life, there is someone dreaming you. It is time that you come to the great cave in the west and meet your sacred dreamer, Woman at the Edge of Two Worlds."

The next thing I knew, I was sitting on an elk hide in front of a small fire on the floor of a womblike cave. Across from me sat a tall, slender figure shrouded in white, sitting on a red Indian blanket. I could not see her face. I wasn't frightened, but I looked at her, trying to see the identity of the person behind the shroud. She said nothing to me. I could tell it was a woman. I sensed femaleness. Then I looked at the floor of the cave and realized that there were inscriptions and symbols and lines drawn everywhere. They shimmered and I realized that the lines were made of mica, glowing and dancing in the firelight. On the walls of the cave were niches with candles, giving a warm radiance to the cavern. Bundles of herbs, rattles, old shields, drums, and sacred bundles of all kinds hung from the ceiling. It was a most magical cave.

"Look closely at the symbols on the floor," a female voice from behind the shroud said to me gently.

I began to look at the symbols on the floor and realized with awe and surprise that they were my own symbols, symbols that I had created in my life and in my gourd. I saw horses, for instance. Horses were a symbol of freedom, of growth, of power for me, of beauty. I saw horses everywhere, and then I realized that the floor had been separated into pieces like a puzzle, that on my left were symbols from my earliest childhood. As I looked at the symbols, I got up and walked around them in excitement, saying, "But this is my childhood." As I expressed these feelings, the words I spoke were formed into actual pictures in front of me. Everything that I was thinking, that I was saying, suddenly showed up in pictures before my eyes.

"Do not be afraid," the woman said. "Simply move into the magical process that is in front of you, just as you do in life. Take what comes and do not be afraid. What you think is what you create."

And truly, I was not afraid. I was not the person any longer who had entered the cave. I was different. Suddenly, everything was envisioned in front of me like a hologram of light—every thought, every word. I wish I could explain the power of the experience. Imagine, if you think of your mother and suddenly she's in front of you in radiant light, and then you move your thought to food and the food is emblazoned in front of you. Every picture in my mind existed life-size, flash after flash, before my eyes. Suddenly the cave was filled with thought forms, and I realized for the first time in my life how cluttered our minds are. I could see that the roof chatter of my brain filled my life with confusion and distracted me from what is really true and needed.

"That is the first lesson of the gateway," the woman said, still behind the shroud of shimmering white material. She was reading my mind and its pictures, just as I read my thoughts as they appeared in front of me.

I took a deep breath and tried to clear my mind, to let my thoughts die down so that I could begin to examine the puzzle on the floor. I walked around carefully, feeling the quality of the smooth earth beneath my feet. I went over to a piece of puzzle that represented my life in Massachusetts when I was about four years old. I saw myself walking through stalks of corn with my father, and I heard my mother's voice calling from the kitchen. The scene brought up enormous grief inside me, the grief for a lost family, a lost experience. My mind shifted to Seattle, Washington. I saw Lake Washington spread out before me and Meydenbauer Bay where I had spent so many of my early days. I saw the high pine trees and felt the wind in my hair. I sat at the end of the dock, both a sad child and an ecstatic child alternately. I realized that all of my life, and for the first time I saw this clearly, my mind took me away from my own happiness, from my joy, from the extraordinary bliss that is in my spirit. Always my mind pulled me away from that experience, my mind full of ego and worry and pain. I realized that it is the nature of people to experience this. I was thankful, and I knelt down on that piece of puzzle that looked like Lake Washington and I gave a prayer of thanks to the Great Spirit and to the great Earth Mother who were helping me to see this with clarity for the first time.

"How simple it all really is," I said out loud.

In front of me I saw a beautiful desert plain in Arizona. It represented simplicity to me. I laughed and the veiled woman took off a layer of her shroud and the shadow of her face became clearer. I thought to myself, How silly we are as human beings to complicate life that is so truly simple. Stay with the essence of your being. And I began to laugh like I have never laughed. I thought of the old Kuna Indian woman, Twin Dreamers the shape shifter, and suddenly she was in front of me—Twin Dreamers with her hair in knots, twigs sticking out in all directions, her gnarled fingers patting me on the shoulder, giving me her wisdom and encouragement.

"Twin Dreamers, you heal with humor. You taught me so much, and you still teach me so much. Why is it that I take myself so seriously?"

Twin Dreamers slapped her knees and laughed, and she said, "Because you think you're so important." And I laughed with her, because it was the truth.

"Righteousness," the lady in the veil said, "self-righteousness."

I said, "Yes, I have always needed to be right, haven't I? I wanted so much to emulate truth in some way."

Twin Dreamers laughed uproariously at this statement. She pinched my cheek. She said, "Little Wolf, we are all so important and we are all nothing. Say, 'I am nothing,' my daughter," she said.

I took a deep breath and said, "I am nothing."

Again Twin Dreamers laughed uproariously. "See," she said, "and all of it is true. You are everything and you are nothing. As we move through the gateway of initiation," she said, "you will begin to see the importance of your unimportance."

I took a deep breath. Part of me wanted to resist what she was saying, because still my ego wanted to feel important. I looked down again at the puzzle on the floor. Twin Dreamers walked over to a certain piece, and with her walking stick, she was tapping away, wanting my attention. She was nodding her head, twirling her head around like an owl, and waiting for my attention. I walked over to the piece of puzzle that she was indicating, and I saw my father and my mother as I had known them as a young child. I saw them arguing as they had argued so many years ago, my father in a fury, frightening me, scaring me half to death. Twin Dreamers began to laugh. I realized something that I was finding hard to explain to myself, that somehow this teaching about my parents had created a teaching for my whole life, and the teaching essentially was that we think our particular conditioning is so important to who we are or become. I had experienced tension as a child and equated that feeling with love. I saw how unconsciously I looked for tension as an adult to re-create that distorted feeling of what I had thought love was, like a child who is beaten and grows up and marries someone who beats her. It is not only familiar. The beating, in a confused way, produces an emotion that we think is love. We spend so many hours of a day, so many hours of our lives, re-creating conditioning of childhood.

"When you react, you're dead. When you act, you're alive," Twin Dreamers said as she tapped a piece of the puzzle again, and I saw a knot envisioned in front of me, being pulled tight, squeaking from the tightness, and I thought, Yes, Twin Dreamers, you're right, tension. Tension was my experience as a child, tension and fear.

Suddenly I saw myself teetering at the edge of the Grand Canyon, my toes over the edge of the cliff, dangerously close to falling into the abyss. I laughed. "Yes, I often feel at the edge of the abyss," I said.

Twin Dreamers laughed again. She said, "See, see what a teaching this is, my daughter. You believe it, don't you? But see? See in front of you the illusions of light. Are they not real?"

And I looked at pictures of my childhood, one after another. I said, "Yes, they are real. They *are* real."

Then suddenly I saw pictures in the north direction of the cave, of anger. I saw fires burning in buildings, men and women screaming, looting, angry on the streets, tearing apart their city. The anger is in all of us for the inequities that we believe to be so real, that in fact are real. The pain is felt, but pain is felt because of our attitudes toward life, because of our inability to be in touch with our own sacred truth. I saw that and thought how inadequate words are to describe this feeling. There are no words; there are no words to describe what is real and what is truth.

Twin Dreamers came over to me and gave me a hug. I smelled cedar in her hair, the breath of the north wind surrounding us with the scent of pine and the high mountain peaks where she mostly lived. Then as quickly as she had appeared in front of me, she disappeared, and I got down on my hands and knees and examined the rest of the floor of the cave, the pictures of my childhood, my adolescence, and all of my adult life and my marriages and the pain and the joy. I saw the birth and life of my beautiful child. And I laughed. I laughed a laughter that was not at anyone or even at myself, but a laughter of understanding the place of all things, the order and the teachings that had been a part of my early life.

Finally, I went back to the fire and sat across from the shrouded woman. I felt a need to be quiet, a need to meditate. I had been cleansed in a way, and as I thought that, the woman got up from the other side of the flames, and she walked around sunwise to me. Taking my hand, she had me rise.

"Remove my veils," she said. I stood up slowly, my hands trembling. I felt the gossamer material, soft, silken between my fingers, and with excitement I slowly lifted the veil and arranged it behind the head of Woman at the Edge of Two Worlds. At first the radiance of her face blinded my eyes. "Soften your vision," she said. "Don't give away your power—remember who you are."

She was a most extraordinary woman. She was not young and she was not old. I could not tell what nationality she was. She seemed to encompass all of what is female. Her face was so very beautiful to look at. She wore a crown of flowers around her head. She held intelligence in her gaze. She was dressed simply in flowing cloth that seemed to hold gold and silver light from the sun and the moon. She was like an angel to me, and I felt an extraordinary depth of love for her and coming from her heart. She put her arms around me and she held me, as I had so often imagined the Great Mother holding me in her arms. I felt a comfort like no other. It was then for the first time that I understood the need for comforting as I moved through this gateway, and I knew that she understood all of my strengths and my frailties.

"When your heart beats, it is the pulsation of the Great Goddess Mother's heart. You are the one, and you are one with all that lives. When you breathe, it is the Great Spirit who breathes. When you grieve, it is the Goddess Spirit that grieves. When you bleed, it is Mother Earth who bleeds, and when you hold your power and your blood, it is the Goddess Spirit of wise-blood becoming whole within you. You are a wise one now. Take this experience of me unto yourself and fill the sacred gourd womb of your sisters' with new wisdom and knowledge of a better way to live."

We stood for some time together, and then she backed away from me and placed her hand on my belly, and she said, "You hold the ancient marriage basket, the ancient clay pot, the ancient gourd of fertility within you. It is your womb, and within this womb the possibilities of all creation exist."

Woman at the Edge of Two Worlds knelt down and she picked up a gourd, a beautiful gourd. It was my gourd, which had been painted with symbols and hung with feathers. Holding the gourd next to my belly, she said, "This represents the new aspect of your womb. This is the ancient life-giver and holder of wise-blood within sisterhood cultures that have lived on this earth forever. Take this ancient gourd and let it be your womb. Now look inside." She took the top and lifted it away. "Let the gourd hear your voice. Look into the gourd and see the future. Do not repeat the inequities of the past, for the future holds all truth for you."

I looked into the gourd and I saw images of life—trees, healthy and strong, the Arizona desert, and the citadels of wisdom, saguaro cactus, standing guard over the desert floor. I saw the guardians of my own spirit, the great wolf spirits running free in the northern territories. As I looked into the gourd, I heard the sound of my own voice coming from a pond in the north. I saw the revelation of my own spirit in peace and harmony. Perhaps for the first time in my life, I felt a sense of security that at last there really was someone for me, to stand with me, and it was Woman at the Edge of Two Worlds.

"Form a sisterhood," she said. "Form a sisterhood of all women, for no matter where you come from or who you are or what your walk of life, when you move through the gateway of Changing Woman, you move through a gateway that all sisters move through. It is a commonality—it is the beginning of your sacred life and your true sisterhood on earth."

With these words I took the top of the gourd and replaced it. I held up the gourd, honoring the Great Mother and the goddess figures that surrounded us in spirit in this cave of initiation. Then turning to this great guide, this great teacher, Woman at the Edge of Two Worlds, I thanked her for all that she had given me. I thanked her for her knowledge and her wisdom, and I promised to take this wisdom and this new aspect of my life-giving womb to my sisters.

"You will hear my voice, my daughter, and you will see my face in all the named and nameless things. Listen well, for I am here for you and all who pass my way." Her voice was like a whisper on the wind as she slowly disappeared from view.

20

MOON FIRE

*S*everal days had gone by since our initiation with Woman at the Edge of Two Worlds and our parting ceremony. These were days of reflection and long walks with my teachers. On my last night Agnes, Ruby, July, Olivia, and I were seated around a bonfire in a clearing in the wilderness. The moon was rising full and yellow behind the towering pines. We were playing our drums and singing in ceremony to Grandmother Moon. It was a moon ceremony dedicated to the power of woman and wise-blood. I offered my menstrual cycle, the end of my moon, my periods as I had known them, to her. We danced around the fire late that night, holding our moon shields first to the fire, honoring the council flames that leapt into the air, orange and yellow with flashes of blue, and then we held our shields to the moon, honoring the grandmother transiting the sky, honoring Grandmother Moon, who lives within our own bodies.

It was almost dawn when we covered the fire with moist juniper branches and then lifted them away so that the smoke could rise into the night air. Olivia and I had placed prayers in the flames to Woman at the Edge of Two Worlds. She had initiated us well into the sacred caves of second life. Both of us saw and knew her differently, and only in a sacred way did we speak of our meetings with her. Olivia had traveled the dimensions of her initiation in the talons of an eagle. She was joyous, and yet unable to tell us all what had transpired. We watched the smoke for the answers to our prayers, to our questions. The smoke curled in gray, plumelike designs over our heads, and then it circled around us like giant dancing kachinas in a waking dream. In the center of the fire was a lavender color telling us that power was here. It suddenly made itself known in crackling sparks from the dying embers.

Suddenly, I could see the face of Woman at the Edge of Two Worlds—her ancient, beautiful face, looking down at me from the clouds of smoke. I could hear her voice saying to me, "My daughter, your sacred life, your true sacred path, has just begun."

21

REENTRY

Shortly after, excited and tired, I drove for several hours across the windswept plains to the airport. It was dawn of the next morning before I sat on the flight to Los Angeles, exhausted and drinking a ginger ale and eating peanuts. The plane was over-crowded except for my three-seat row. Somehow I managed to be sitting alone. I wondered where all these people came from at such an early hour. Three small children sat just in front of me. One was noisily flipping his chair seat back and forth. The other two were screaming, beating each other with plastic rattles. They were unattended. The frazzled stewardess was standing over me silently mouthing the words of a male voice coming over the loudspeaker, giving flight instructions. She dangled a yellow Dixie cup attached to clear plastic tubes and bounced it off my nose, knocking my glasses to the floor.

"Sorry. Oxygen . . . " she said, continuing to mime the directions.

"I need some," I said. My stomach suddenly gave me a wrenching pain. The sudden jolt of noisy humanity and air travel was getting to me. I sniffed the back of my hand in hopes of finding the scent of sweetgrass or cedar from the fire, but only the scent of lavatory soap remained.

A gray haired man across from me peered over his coke-bottle thick spectacles. He growled at me, holding a paperback book with huge lettering out at arm's length. "Hard to stomach the situation, huh?"

I looked at him through red, swollen eyes that had not experienced sleep in days and grunted a quiet animal sound, nodding my head, as he resubmerged into his prime-time fiction. After-ceremony-let-down, like a dense tule fog, settled over me.

Trying to regain the feeling of exultation and my awe for the wondrous mysteries of life, I thought of horses and Tsunami, the Arabian stallion that I had seen in Phoenix, Arizona, a few months before. He was one of the most beautiful and charismatic horses I have ever known. It had been a few years since I had seen him, and I had waited with great expectation that day at the stable to see him come out of his stall with his groom. Instead of the great stallion I remembered, what came toward me was a ghost horse that for some reason instantly reminded me of the current situation in the world, especially America. I wanted to cry when I saw Tsunami. His eyes were still bright, his spirit was still proud and strong, but his body, recovering from a severe colic operation, was swaybacked, making his imperfect legs stand out even more. It was as if they had gotten worse, as if he didn't have a leg to stand on—like America, spavined and low in the back from corruption, so far off the mark in so many important ways that she is losing her stature in the world community.

So many emotions and thoughts pressed through my mind and heart as I watched the once-great stallion. I must have looked odd just standing there shaking my head. I had thought at the time, Am I so off balance with my chaotic hormones that everything quakes my interior Richter scale off the graph? I simply sat down in the dirt and shavings of the aisle and watched the old boy arch his neck as a big-eyed bay mare looked his way through the metal grating of her stall. Tsunami squealed a little and tried to rear and puff up his shoulders, as if he were heroically sucking in his girth, but he gave up and took a few prancing steps instead. Oh God, I thought, that's what we all do, isn't it, as we get older—we take a few prancing steps instead.

I must have dozed off for hours, because I awoke in disbelief as we touched down with a gentle bounce. I looked out across the vast expanse of Los Angeles' houses, glass windows shining in the filtered sunlight, smog mixing with the afternoon mist from the ocean, leaving a residue of tannish brown cloud into which I was plunging. The ceremonies of the nights before were imprinted deeply into my heart. I wondered how I could impart the essence of those ceremonies to the women I work with in Los Angeles. I was filled with excitement and enthusiasm at the thought of being able to share this ancient knowledge with my sisters.

As I moved out of the baggage claim area, my senses were shattered by the loud honking of taxi horns and people yelling and shoving. I was struck by the many races that were represented around me. Los Angeles has changed so much in the last ten years. I felt that I was in a foreign country. In a way, that was very wonderful, because it meant that at last we were moving into an age when we will, indeed, all be of one race.

It was good to get to my peaceful home that afternoon. My house was quiet, and I set out my sacred things on my altar. I had made arrangements for everyone to leave me alone this night, so that I could crawl into bed and reenter Los Angeles peacefully. I was exhausted and fell into a deep sleep, and I dreamed of Agnes and Ruby and the northern lights.

The next morning I was awakened by the phone at eight o'clock. I had a headache and jet lag and stumbled out of bed, lurched into the bathroom, and looked at myself for several minutes trying to remember where I was. Images of Agnes's cabin in Manitoba, Canada, maneuvered through my mind as I opened the drawers and brushed my teeth.

Again the phone rang. I answered.

"Lynn, I'm so glad you're home. We have a meeting at five o'clock today with the producers of the Expo in San Francisco," said Ann's cheerful voice. She is my producer for my shaman training in the spring.

"Oh, hi, Ann. So good to hear your voice. Five o'clock? Who are we meeting?"

"You know, Jeff from the Expo in San Francisco. We need to talk about the booth and . . . " Her voice went on as my thoughts moved back to the moon ceremony. For a moment I could see the flames jumping in front of me and the face of Woman at the Edge of Two Worlds. I placed my hands on the tile counter in front of me, feeling its coolness, reassuring myself that I was still in the real world. I took a deep breath, centering myself, and laughed.

"What are you laughing at?" Ann said.

"Oh, nothing, I'm just trying to get myself back into Los Angeles."

"Yes, it must be difficult for you. Forgive me," she said. "Did you have a good time? How was the weather?"

"It was wonderful," I said, not knowing what else to say, not wanting to sound stupid or as incoherent as I felt. "All right. Where are we meeting at five?"

"At the top of the hill?" Ann said.

"Yes, that will be fine—at the deli. I'll see you at five."

I hung up gratefully, taking another deep breath as the phone rang again. It was my lawyer wanting to know if I had received the contracts for my next book. I hadn't, and I looked at the clock, wondering where my secretary was. She was supposed to have been here a half an hour ago. I could feel the tension mounting inside me as I washed my face and splashed cold water on my neck and shoulders.

Outside it had begun to rain.

22

THE ABYSS OF FEAR

The next afternoon I watched with concern as Beth began to fidget in front of me anxiously pursing and biting her lips.

"Beth, you need to tell me something. What is it you are afraid to say to me?"

"I was at my doctor's yesterday, and he said that I have a condition of early bone loss. I'm frightened and I don't know what it means."

"Look at how you are sitting," I said to her.

Beth looked down. Her shoulders were slumped forward and her chest was concave.

"What are you thinking?"

"I feel," she said in a weak voice, "kind of defeated. Not only can I not have children, but now I am falling apart from the inside out."

I looked at her for a long time and saw her aura retracting, her energy field becoming smaller and smaller. "What are you afraid of, Beth?"

"I'm afraid of being weak and wrong."

"Wrong about what?" I asked.

"I guess I'm afraid of just being wrong. No matter how good I have become, no matter how well I have taken care of my people, my family, I am wrong somehow. How could my body be defeating me like this?"

"Defeating you?" I said. "What do you mean, defeating you? Perhaps your body is trying to tell you something."

"I've been listening," Beth said, "but I don't hear anything."

"Well, maybe you aren't listening well enough," I said. "There is something that you have not learned in your life, something that you have not listened to and that you've avoided with everything that you are. I'm going to end this work for today, and I want you to go home and think about it. Go into your sacred witness and listen carefully, because you're going to come up with it. Don't think this is just something I need to tell you. That's all. I'll see you when you call me."

Beth was not prepared to leave me. She had wanted to stay with me a lot longer, and she was upset that I sent her away. She was even more slump shouldered as she left, carrying her duffel bag, her eyes cast to the ground. She did not look at me.

A week later she called me and we met again in the meadow. This time her stride was more defiant as she walked. I was pleased with how much straighter she was walking. We gave each other a hug and walked down by the river. We sat there in the sacred circle, and we talked for some time. I looked at her quizzically at one point, waiting.

"Well, I learned a lot this last week," Beth said. "I learned more than I have learned in a long time."

"What is that?"

"I learned that I have absolutely never stood up for what I believe in. I never stood up for what I wanted, for what I needed, or anything else." This time Beth did not cry. She was sitting straight.

"Look how you're sitting," I said, "how straight you are. Isn't that interesting?"

"Yes, it is interesting," she said. "It's as if I've taken a stand within myself for the first time, and it seems that all it really took was realizing that I hadn't been standing in a position of power, even within myself, let alone the world."

"Oh, really," I said.

"It is very difficult for me to realize and admit to myself how weak I have been. I can hardly believe it," she said.

I smiled and reached out to her. "Go on, tell me more."

"Something was happening to me. Suddenly at thirty-five I felt ancient. Menopause meant that I was over the hill. I was old."

"Old and decrepit," I said, remembering my conversation with Agnes.

"Oh, yes, I guess so," Beth said, glowing with youth.

"Well, what are you going to do about it?"

"I wanted to talk to you about it," she said. "I was so surprised. I thought that in working with you I was taking my power."

"It's true, Beth. You were taking the first steps, but that isn't enough, is it?"

"No," she said.

"Now you have to act upon that decision, not only in your life, but within your own body."

"I haven't been exercising," she said. "That's one of the main things I realized. I have always been athletic. Suddenly with menopause it was like I was treating myself as if I had a disease. The symptoms were hot flashes and bone loss. I was suddenly becoming careful physically. Instead of running a mile, I would run half a mile."

"Yes," I said, "I know what you mean."

"Did you do that too?" she asked.

"Yes, for a while. Not only did I do that, but I started apologizing for who I was. If Agnes was really strong with me or someone in business was, I would apologize, because I thought I was wrong. I had to be wrong. Wasn't I wrong? But as a matter of fact, I wasn't wrong. They were most of the time. That does not mean that you cannot have an incorrect day, but it does mean that you don't assume that you're wrong until you really are."

Beth opened up a peanut butter and jelly sandwich and gave me half. We sat there eating and talking about this phenomenon of menopause and the sisterhood that it was creating between all of us.

"You know, it doesn't mean that menopause isolates you from younger women or women who went through menopause years before," I said. "It's that you begin to realize that we have such a community because of the fact that we all experience similar things in our lives. Women will eventually stick together. They will learn about sisterhood. They will not lose each other over the competition for men or higher paying jobs. They will support each other in becoming more successful, not only in their relationships, but in their work as well. What I want you to see most of all, Beth, is that you are beginning to exhibit bone loss because you have denied that shadow warrior inside yourself, the killer, the one who will stand up and fight for what she believes in, for who she is, for that magnificent warrior that you are as a woman."

"Yes," Beth said. "It doesn't mean that I can't be passionate and beautiful and soft and loving when I need to be, but it means that I can stand in my essence, in my power, whether I am an elder or a young girl. It doesn't matter. I can shine with my wisdom in the world. Not only will I teach myself, but I will teach other women. In being strong, I can still be loved. You know something, Lynn, something really interesting happened. My husband has a new light in his eyes, and it is the light of respect. It just happened in this last week. It's funny, because as I've stood in my own power, I don't have to nag at him, I'm finding. I don't have to do the things I used to do, because the nagging at him was usually out of my own frustration for myself when I wasn't accomplishing, when I wasn't owning what was in me."

"Ho," I said. "Yes, Beth, that's what I wanted you to find last time when I let you go home upset that I had terminated our time together. I wanted you to think and I wanted you to be angry, because that awakens your will." I placed my hand over her belly. "There, right there, didn't you feel that when you left last week?"

"Yes, I did. I felt that anger, but you know what? It was good for me. I flailed around for days in total confusion, and then suddenly the timing was right and my defenses snapped. I saw what you've been trying to teach me for a year. It woke up something inside me."

"Yes, it was your sacred witness. She woke up and said, 'Ah, there's work to be done.'"

"Yes, that's it."

"There's work to be done, and the best is yet to come."

AROUSAL OF THE INNER FIRE

~~~~~~~~~~~~~~~~~~~~~~~~~~~~~

REKINDLING THE HEAT
OF EARLIER MENOPAUSE

~~~~~~~~~~~~~~~~~~~~~~~~~~~~~

"When I have gone and the fire is only an ember in your memory, you learn to visit me again. Power will come back through your loins and up your spine. There will be an arousal of the inner fire. You will see my face again. For the alchemy to be complete, we must ride as one. Woman at the Edge of Two Worlds visits you as you move and work your magic on earth. You will love, and through love, you will melt into me and we will become as one with all that is sacred."

Slowly the great goddess circled the fire. She became more and more transparent, until the outline of her figure merged with the dancing flames and she was gone.

23

INITIATION

I had been preparing my apprentices for the ceremony to meet Woman at the Edge of Two Worlds for a long time. It seemed like only a day ago that I had experienced the face of Woman at the Edge of Two Worlds instead of the several weeks it had been. Now in a different way I would bring my apprentices who were going through the Changing Woman gateway into this experience.

As I have explained so often, my teachers, two of them, are Native American, but because they are not traditional Native American medicine women, because they have learned an ancient system and process of knowledge embodied in the teachings of the Sisterhood of the Shields, their initiations are different, perhaps, than many Native American nations in North America or South America. Their initiation into wise-blood is a different one. Many of the initiations in ancient societies have been forgotten around the world. Ours have been memorized and held in secret by our shaman women. When the Sisterhood of the Shields initiated me, I was initiated as a west person, and the great dreaming bear took me into the cave of the Great Goddess. It was a teaching for a shaman woman who lives in the twentieth century, a teaching specifically for me. When I work with people, oftentimes the initiations shift and change for the people who are participating. All people should be given a rite of passage or an initiation into their sacred time.

The women that I had been working with—Phyllis, Mary, Linda, Beth, and, of course, Olivia, who is Zoila's apprentice from Central America—were from different heritages, each from a different walk of life, and yet all four were similar in their needs at this particular time in their own personal history. They shared a common ground called menopause. I had worked with them differently, because each needed different aspects of training, and most of that training had to do with peeling away early life conditioning—much like peeling away the layers of an onion skin—underneath which was the core of their being, a state of emptiness and perfection and pure, radiant light. Each of these women had different manifestations of dis-ease relative to the world that she lived in. Each woman had her own difficulties with menopause. Those difficulties existing within her self-wound held the seeds of knowledge and wisdom, planted there for her learning and evolvement in her future life. That is the teaching and the work of the shaman—to enable you to move into the core, into the essence of your being, into the pain most hidden, most secret. Find the essence of a person and you find a teaching for a lifetime. The conflicts at the center of a person's consciousness are the seeds of power and knowledge through which that person is liberated into a true sense of peace, into the true manifestation of their own personal dream in this life.

My four women had not met each other until we got to the high desert plateau in southern California. There's a sacred cave in this area that the women of the Sisterhood and I have used for many years. It was shown to me originally by Twin Dreamers, and in those earlier days I only could experience certain perimeters of that cave, because it was the cave in which women going through this particular gateway of menopause met Woman at the Edge of Two Worlds. This great goddess has many abodes throughout the earth, and she visits them on nights of initiation and has done so for centuries. This is an ancient initiation, and each and every one of the women with me would be seeing her face in a different way. These teachings move you into that interior space of magic and power within yourself. These are the teachings of the ancients. No matter what religion, no matter what nationality, the greatest teachings always move you into a place of power within yourself. You do not place power outside yourself. Truth is a reflection of the Great Spirit, always living within your own heart.

Great brown sand-colored boulders, as if tumbled from a giant's medicine bag a hundred millennia ago, sat around us in a silent reflection of energy and power. We had walked into a sacred canyon, my four apprentices and I. We were wearing long white dresses representing purity of spirit, red sashes representing sacred blood, and shawls showing a position of apprenticeship. The shawls were different: I had asked each woman to wear her favorite shawl. Phyllis and Mary had worn silk shawls of red, splashed with yellow and blue. Linda wore a shawl woven of black wool with threads of gold, and Beth wore a shawl of red raw silk threaded with black ribbon.

The sky that day had been a brilliant cobalt blue, now turning to midnight blue. It was a perfect evening for our ceremony. The waning moon was above us, and we greeted her and each other with prayer and chanting. Then I gave each of the women a torch that had been prepared for us earlier. As we stood at the entrance of the ancient sacred cave, a Joshua tree in front of it and clumps of cholla and yellow and blue wildflowers growing out of the rock crevasses around the mouth of the cave, I lit the torches they held, and we stood in a circle.

"Beth, you hold the direction of the south. You are my south woman in this ceremony. You hold the energy and the power of trust and innocence, of substance and physicalness in the world. You understand the stones that rise to the sky around us. You understand that they hold memories and are the storytellers.

You, Beth, are the storyteller of this circle. You know that many have walked here before us, and you honor them. You hold the power of that direction in this ceremony, and if you find that any one of us forgets about substance, about trust and innocence, about the little child in each of us, you need to voice your opinion."

I lit her torch, and I turned to the west.

"Linda, you are my west woman. You are the holder of the sacred dream. You understand death and rebirth and transformation on all of its levels. You can dance with the sacred dreaming bear. You hold this position of power in our sacred circle. When we forget the adolescent self within and her needs, you voice your opinion. Hold your power well, dear sister."

Then I lit her torch and turned to the north.

"Phyllis, you are the north woman in our ceremony of initiation. You stand in the position of strength and wisdom, the great buffalo, the place of prayer and spirit. You hold that position within our ceremony, and if that place of power is forgotten, let your voice be heard."

I lit her torch as she held it up to the night sky, the waning moon even more brilliant against the flickering stars that surrounded her. Then I moved to the east.

"Mary, you are my east woman in this ceremony. You, though you are so young, hold the power of the old wise one, of illumination. You are the sacred clown in this ceremony. You can voice your opinion. You are the one who tests existing institutions to see if they are real. You understand the power of the rising sun and her radiance. I honor you, east sister. If you find there is something lacking in the power of the east, voice your opinion and it will be heard."

I lit her torch. It burst into flames. Then I asked all of them to sit in a circle around me. I sat in the position of the self in the center. I said a prayer to the Great Spirit.

"Great Spirit, Mother Earth, powers of the four directions, my ancestors, my medicine, the four leggeds and the winged ones, and all the sacred beings and teachers that walk this earth, I honor you, and I ask you all to be with us here tonight."

I rang a bell four times for the four directions, and I called in the spirit of my guardians and all those who love me and the members of my circle. Taking my mother rattle, I stood and with a halo of sound, beginning with my south woman, Beth, I called in her guardians and her power animal. I moved to the west and the north and the east, honoring the sacred directions and their power, and I invoked their presence into our circle.

Then I asked the women to stand, and using a stack of fire sticks, I ignited a small fire that had been prepared near the center of our circle. I gave each of them a fire stick, which I had threaded with the colors of the powerful fire from within of each of the four women. I asked them to do a cleansing ceremony with that stick, imaging their negativity moving into that fire stick as they ran it from the top of their heads, down their arms, down the trunk of their bodies and their backs and their legs and their feet.

"Let the fire stick absorb your negativity," I said. "Let the fire stick absorb the unwanted baggage of your life up until now. You know through our work together what you have accomplished and what no longer serves you. Let what no longer serves you move into the fire stick. Let the fire stick take it. It can handle it much better than you can. Give it away to the fire before you move into the sacred cave with me."

Each woman ran a fire stick over her body. The threads that I had twisted around the ends shone brilliantly in the firelight. It was now completely dark outside. The smell of sand and wildflowers floated on the desert wind, filling our nostrils with a scent of wilderness and the fragrance of our great earth mother. As each woman had finished with her fire stick, she threw that fire stick into the fire in the center of the circle.

"Now kneel," I instructed. "Kneel in front of the fire and say a prayer. See how the flames transform the wood to smoke, just as your inner heat transforms your body into a new state of perfection. Say a prayer to the Great Spirit and the great mothers that surround us, and ask them for strength and energy during your initiation. Ask for guidance in the new life that you are about to begin." Then I placed juniper branches that had been watered down onto the fire. The flames sizzled and sparked and a great cloud of smoke lifted into the night sky. "Spirit and the central fire will speak to you through the smoke," I said. "Read the pictures in the smoke for guidance." The smoke snaked about us in undulating plumes of lavender and gray. Each of us read profound messages in the silent dance of the smoke.

When each of the women was finished, we walked clockwise around the circle. I blessed each woman with sage and cedar and sweetgrass. Then I led the way into the sacred cave. The cave opening was just high enough to admit us, and as we entered we passed the great boulder that I had rolled away from the entrance. We could smell earth and the ancient stone walls. As I walked I lit candles that were set in crevasses and niches along our path.

As we walked I said, "Women, hold your torches high in your left hand, the hand of female power, the hand of true power. You are the torchbearers for all women who walk after you who will celebrate the gateway of menopause as a movement forward into their sacred lives."

We walked slowly. The pathway led gently downward, deeper and deeper into Mother Earth. As we moved downward, the path began to spiral around to the right like a nautilus shell, down and down into the heart of the earth. It became cooler and cooler with each step. We walked carefully and for a long while, as I lit the candles placed along the path. The faces of my apprentices were shining with anticipation as occasionally I would look toward them. Then we began to smell the scent of sweetgrass and the pungent scent of wood fire ahead of us. As we turned a graceful corner in the hallway of the cave, the ceiling just high enough for us to stand erect, we saw ahead of us a brilliant circumference of light. We walked into a cavernous room, the ceiling domed high above us, carved seemingly out of a giant boulder. There was a fire set in the floor of the cavern, sacredly lit and ceremonially blessed. The walls of the cave shone like burnished gold, because of the tiny sheets and flecks of mica gleaming like polished silver and gold, and reflected the spiral yellow light of the fire as if the sun shone with hot intensity from within it. Beautiful designs were etched into the stone floor. The cavelike room was awaiting our initiation.

In the center of the room was a grand jaguar chair carved out of stone. The seat was the back of the jaguar. The arms of the chair were jaguars lying lengthwise, their faces looking toward us, their eyes set with mica, reflecting the jumping flames of the central fire, as if they were alive. The back of the chair was carved out of stone, fashioned with snakes and cobras. The face of a beautiful goddess figure was imprinted into the stone at the top of the back of the chair. I moved around the cavern, leading them counterclockwise.

"We will move in this direction, my sisters. This is the direction of ordinary power."

After we had moved completely around the cavern, we reversed and I led them in the other direction.

"This is the direction of magical female power," I said as we moved around sunwise to the right. "Take your position now around the room in your sacred direction." The women situated themselves on sacred red blankets in the four directions and placed their torches in holders dug into the stone floor of the cave.

I went to the chair, and walking around it four times, I blessed it with sage, cedar, and sweetgrass. Then, standing in front of the chair, I chanted and sang my power song. Picking up a drum and rattles that were set nearby, I began to play the drum, and I sang an ancient song that my teachers had taught me for the invocation of Woman at the Edge of Two Worlds. The goddess felt close to me now, so it was proper and fitting to call in her presence at this time. After a short period of time, I began to see her face well. Then I sat on the chair facing the fire, and ringing a bell, I again called her in to join us. As I prayed I saw clearly Woman at the Edge of Two Worlds, her ancient but beautiful face emerging out of the smoke from the fire and the copal incense smoldering nearby. Her face glowed with power and strength, and she reached out to me and touched my third eye.

"I am grateful to you, my daughter, for bringing these beautiful women to me. I bless your ceremony and I bless your apprentices with power. I will help them in their sacred life. I will be there for them as I am there for you. In light and honor walk in beauty all the days of your life. Ho," she said and slowly disappeared into the haze created in the room by the smoking copal, sage, and sweetgrass.

I got up and said, "Beth, south woman, I will ask you to begin. Will you come, please, and join me here on the jaguar seat, the place of forgetting and remembering, a place of great honor."

Beth got up and moved with strength, proudly, across the designs on the floor of the cavern. There were many lines drawn, as if she were walking across the universe with the Pleiades, the sun, and grandmother moon drawn beneath her feet. She sat down carefully in the chair. I could tell that it felt comfortable to her. She placed her hands on the arms of the chair. Her hands fit perfectly into the indentations made by so many other women who had been there before her. I reached up and covered her head and entire body with a white sheer-cotton cloth that had been folded neatly under the chair.

"I cover you with a veil. It is a veil of innocence befitting your direction. It is a veil of ignorance, a symbol for what has clouded your vision in your past life up until now. I would like you to express to Woman at the Edge of Two Worlds and to all of us an invocation for power. I would like you to tell us what the passing through this gateway means to you and what you are leaving behind so that your rebirth and transformation can be complete."

From a basket woven from the dreams of all women and heaped with offerings, I took an offering for Beth. I gave her a sacred gourd, symbolizing her newly realized womb of creativity, to hold in her left hand and tobacco to hold in her right hand.

"The gourd represents the fecundity of your spirit, the wealth of the seeds planted within your own being that bring you to this moment of initiation. The tobacco represents a way of bringing messages to the Great Goddess Mother and the Great Spirit. It offers you a way to pray and be renewed with energy and power on your path."

For a moment Beth was silent. She held the gourd and the tobacco with dignity, proudly. Then she began to speak and tell us of her determination in what she was giving up so that her initiation could be complete.

"I am a good enemy to those who would wish me harm. I stand in my power, and I give away my fear of being wrong. I give away any fear of making other people upset because of what I believe to be true. I was afraid to have a point of view. I give these millstones of fear away."

When she finished I stood up and placed my hands on either side of her head, and I prayed to Woman at the Edge of Two Worlds to appear to her in all of her radiance and beauty.

"Now, Beth," I said, "ask Woman at the Edge of Two Worlds to teach you and to appear to you. I want you to imagine that you are looking out across the desert, and in the distance you see a figure walking toward you. You realize that it is the great goddess, Woman at the Edge of Two Worlds, coming to you. As she moves closer, you begin to see her in all of her splendor. She reveals herself to you in a very private way. It is a vision that is meant for you and for you only. I will extinguish the torches," I said as I walked around the circle allowing a shadowy darkness to engulf us with mystery. "We will drum now, and when you are finished with your vision, raise your left hand, and we will cease drumming and go on with the ceremony."

I began drumming the heartbeat of Mother Earth. The other

women joined in on their drums. A long time went by and finally Beth raised her left hand, holding the sacred gourd, and we ceased our drumming. I stood up and went to Beth and removed the veil and set it over the back of the chair. Beth's face was radiant. Tears streamed down her cheeks. Her vision and her initiation were complete. She moved back to her position in the south with the vision of her new ally held close inside her. The fire glowed in the center of our circle like the eye of eternal wisdom, watching us with approval and flickering animation.

Linda, from the place of power in the west, moved to the center of the room and the seat of the grand jaguar. We repeated the ceremony. I placed the veil over her and asked her to tell us about her determination and her acts of power for her new life as she walked in sacredness. I asked her to tell us about what she was leaving behind that would keep her from her initiation. I also gave her a sacred gourd and tobacco, and we all listened with great respect as she began to speak.

"I leave behind my racial prejudice. I leave behind the feeling that I'm not good enough to be a senator. I give away my fear of losing my marriage. If my husband is upset about my menopause, that is a problem he needs to overcome. At last I understand fully that a new society of equality cannot be created out of anger, but only from a place of heart."

"If Woman at the Edge of Two Worlds does not feel the truth in your heart, she will not come to you," I said.

When she was finished, again I invoked the spirit of Woman at the Edge of Two Worlds. The goddess came to Linda very quickly, and when she was finished, I lifted her veil and she rejoined the circle. Again the fire seemed to come alive. Tiny flames leapt out from the red hot coals as if acknowledging Linda and her new presence.

Then I asked my north woman, Phyllis, to sit in the center. I gave her a gourd and tobacco and covered her head with the veil. She told us with deep emotion and a strong voice what she was going to give up and about her determination for her new life.

"I am determined to be me and not a shadow of my husband. I was so afraid to be me. I resolve to see the world through my own eyes and not someone else's. I give away all that fear about not being normal or socially correct. I was afraid to dance, but I will dance now and help others to express their deepest truth through rhythmic movement."

When she was finished, I began to drum and together, we invoked the spirit of Woman at the Edge of Two Worlds. We removed her veil and she entered the circle again, truly a new woman. I could see it in the glow in her face, in the radiance of her eyes. She wept soft tears of joy as the fire burst forth with a new intensity, as if we had added more wood.

I asked east woman, Mary, to take the chair, and she was covered with the veil, as the women before her had been. I asked her what she was going to give up and what her resolve was for her new life as a sacred woman. She spoke to us from her heart.

"Asian women, Native American women, Anglo women, African-American women, women from all over the world, all races and all cultures have many things in common. I am just beginning to really feel this. Women understand this. Women understand childbirth. Women understand the nurturing of the family, the protective instinct that nurtures and allows all forms of life to grow. Women bleed; all women together have a period of cleansing every month, and all women go through the change of life. We are bonded together, sisters, all of us, if we will but understand the extraordinary importance of that fact. In my professional life I have found that oftentimes my biggest enemies have been women. It was very difficult for me to understand that early on, because I felt that it was such a natural thing to stand together with other women, to fight for other women so that we would all win, so that we could all be successful. But oftentimes women, in looking out at the patriarch, try to fashion themselves after the people in power, and so often those people in power are men. So they become linear in their thinking and they forget the sacred circle of life. They forget what they know, and they fight sister against sister, never reaching out a hand to help or to give consolation or compassion. I give away the fear of being a sister first, in all the acts in my life."

When Mary was finished, we drummed and called in the presence of Woman at the Edge of Two Worlds. All of us could feel her, each of us seeing her in our own way, each of us full of emotion and empowered beyond anything that we had remembered. I removed Mary's veil, and she rejoined the circle. We sang and prayed together and chanted and drummed.

"My teachers have told me often that the hope of the world is with the women of the west," I said, "and more and more I think that that statement has been validated, because women understand the energy of Mother Earth, for after all, she is female. Women also understand each other. They understand about giving life and nurturing that life in an ongoing manner. It is time that we as women bond together on all levels of life, whether it be in the business world, at home, or in the consciousness of healing Mother Earth, so that we all may live, so that our grandchildren all may live in a place of health and harmony and peace. I think if someone were to ask me what the journey through the gateway of Woman at the Edge of Two Worlds has taught me, I would say that it has brought all of this to mind, that women can realize a new basis of understanding that is not only intellectual and emotional, but is part of their bodies, part of what their identity is in the world."

We prayed for several hours. We shared our sisterhood, and we drummed and sang. Then I told my apprentices I had something special for them.

"I have a message for all of you from Agnes Whistling Elk." I closed my eyes and remembered my beautiful elder teacher as she was looking at the passing water of a stream. She had begun to speak very quietly. I said, "I will repeat her words. 'As we women are related to the water, it is good to be near moving water during your moon. We are born of the first words of the first mother. We are of the void and we carry the void. Our blood is her body. It is sacred. It is said she was born of the water and the earth, and that is why your blood shall return to the earth and your spirit to the waters of the sacred dream. Her power shall be honored over all the earth, and all men shall know her as the beginning. And now that you have transformed your body into the womb time, take care that your blood seed of our first mother is welcomed in a sacred way, for it is of her body. Her flesh has been burned that you may be given life. Her smoke will bring wisdom to your way. Smoke is a gift from the first mother's heart. Bless her memory, for she lives within you. When you eat, it is she who eats. When you smoke, it is she who takes your message to the faraway. When you bleed, it is she who bleeds. And when you hold your blood, hold your newfound power, for you now are the great women of wise-blood. When you hold your blood it is she who holds her blood. When you give your body to be divided in love, let all parts of you be in her name so that her love can be complete on this great earth.'" We looked at each other and hugged one another, our eyes full of tears and wonder for the beauty of Agnes's words and gifts to us.

Finally, together, we walked sunwise around the room, the direction of power, and taking our torches that we had left in the holders, I lit them and we moved out of the sacred chamber and back up the tunnel leading again through darkness. This time I walked behind the women, picking up the trail, putting out the candles in the niches as I walked until we reached daylight, the light at the end of the tunnel. Indeed the whole night had passed, and it was dawn and the beginning of a new life for each of us.

24

THE SHADOW WARRIOR OF MENOPAUSE

It was late fall and I sat with my apprentices and Olivia under an oak tree in a meadow full of fragrant purple lantana flowers. Pine trees grew in small tribes over the landscape, and the soft wind coming up from the south whistled through the pine needles, reminding me of the far north and the wilderness I love. It had been some time since we had worked together during our initiation with Woman at the Edge of Two Worlds. The last time we had all been together was at the feast that we gave for all of the members of our families. That had been a joyous occasion as we celebrated our initiation, ate together, danced, played drums, and talked. Everyone had simply relaxed and enjoyed themselves fully. The best part was that each one of my apprentices was honored deeply and profoundly by everyone present. What a wonderful experience it had been to feel the love and see the respect on the faces of those families.

We sat in a circle on colorful red, blue, yellow, and white blankets talking about our "animal dreams," as we called them, because each of us, since the meeting with that great goddess woman, had been having dreams of our power animals—the animal archetypes that live within our psyche and animate our wild instinctual nature, which we so often deny. Early on in our work together we do ceremony to discover our power animals.

In one dream that Phyllis had, she had seen the Virgin Mary with her foot on the great plumed serpent. She had realized an interesting interpretation of that symbolism. In a sense menopause was a way of leading her back into a feeling of being a virgin, as if the life that she was facing now was fresh, as if she were a nature virgin walking into the world renewed with different eyes. She was a virgin spirit with her foot on the uncontrollable conformity and the perilous mediocrity of her previous life.

Each of us had had dreams of our power animals manifesting themselves in our everyday life. We talked about this for some time, sharing a picnic lunch, laughing and enjoying each other's company. Linda had been given spirit hands by her power animal, a female puma. They were her special secret hands that allowed her to create a new world and "handle" whatever came her way.

Finally, I took the talking stick, held it for a moment to my forehead, to my shaman eye, and closing my eyes, I offered a prayer to the Goddess Mother for her blessings.

"There is something I want to talk to you all about," I said. A blue jay landed on a branch above my head. He seemed to be mimicking my words, jumping around on the branch, trying to get our attention. I threw him a crust from my sandwich.

"There is something that I see in all of you that we have not spoken of before," I said. "I see that you have advanced tremendously. I see that your work with your sacred nature has been most powerful for you. Diving into your self-wound and doing ceremony within your own female power has brought you into the mysteries and magic of a second birth. You are truly changing women in a world that needs to hear your shout for joy. But I think something else has happened that you are not yet aware of. Do you know what that might be?"

I looked at the faces of each of my women. They were thinking deeply, yet nobody came up with an answer.

"Let's call it the shadow side of menopause. There is a shadow side of menopause, the secret depths of confusion that come, per-haps, from not knowing who we are or what we are at this par-ticular time in our lives. The energy is new and you are about to take a new consort into your sacred cave. I think we relate to act-ing in the world as being part of the female shield. We see the process of expression as being part of us as women and how we express that femaleness in the world. But I think, my dear apprentices, that something else is happening here. It was shown to me in my last meeting with Woman at the Edge of Two Worlds that the last initiation that we are going through in this passage is about to take place. It will take place after you leave me and go back to your earth walk."

"I don't understand exactly what you're saying," Phyllis said.

"What I am saying is that there is one thing that we have missed. I call 'whom' we have missed, the *shadow warrior.* You know, menopause can be looked at in so many ways, and I think we have danced around this passage from every direction. But look at the word. Men-o-pause. How does that relate, do you think, to this passage?" I emphasized the syllables.

They thought for several minutes, and Beth, chewing on an end of a piece of grass, looked at me intently and said, "Is it pos-sible that in this passage we carry the female shield, and yet to balance that female shield we need to pick up the male shield? Does it have something to do with that, Lynn?"

"Yes, what is happening is that most of us think that we go out into the world always carrying a female shield, but in actual-ity there is also a *shadow warrior* within each of us. That *shadow warrior* comes out of the male shield, like a mist hover-ing over the lake at dawn, and we have not yet, not any one of us, perceived the vitality of the energy we are all feeling. I see the orange-gold energy glowing around each of you. I think to understand the men-o-pause, we have to pause to consider and reflect upon the *shadow warrior,* that male part that is within us, that at this moment challenges us."

"Before we go on with this discussion," Mary said, "do you

mean that every woman has a *shadow warrior,* and what does a warrior have to do with female blood anyway?"

"Yes to your first question," I said. "That is different from the male shield or male aspect of ourselves that we ordinarily understand. During menopause, to answer your next question, the *shadow warrior* is created when the male shield is not integrated with the female shield and balanced properly. Every woman has a *shadow warrior* from time to time, but that *shadow warrior* does not really make himself known to you until the gateway of Changing Woman. Because a woman goes so deeply inside her female wound at that time, the need for a different kind of balance is born. The *shadow warrior* dances to your song. If you are a woman of power weaving a tapestry of mystery and creativity, he could be the loom that holds your brilliant threads and demonstrates their form in the world. It's not that a woman is formless within her own female shield, but the balance and the force with which her creation is expressed depends upon the eternal matching of positive and negative energy play within the spiral dance of life. The *shadow warrior* is your consort at this time. He holds the lightning flash in his right hand and your bones in his left hand of power. Lightning is the brilliance of the Great Spirit, and together, with your bones, is formed the shield of the *shadow warrior.* He challenges you to be your awesome best. Your life now is a second birth into a sacred time of rebalancing all the energy forms of your life."

Linda took a flower she had in her hair and tossed it into the center of the circle. "Do you mean," she said, "that all men have a *shadow warrior* or *warrioress* as well?"

"That is correct. It means that there is a silent side, a place that remains dormant within each of us. It is a place deep within our history that is held in our blood, like our manifested spirit lives within our bones. When we traverse the sacred Dreamtime, we become a carrier of the Bones of Time. Bone Woman, the Keeper of the Bones, gathers the bones throughout woman's karma of magic and menopause. The last teacher of this gateway of wise-blood is Bone Woman. She holds your bones up to the light of the waning moon, and she reads your spirit and names your state of health and decides your choice of death. As we move through our lifetimes, these places within us, these places of knowledge, hold secrets that are kept from us. The mystery of life is held secret in your blood, until you become wise and know how to use the information. Secrets that might damage our ability to survive, our ability to perceive truth, are held in abeyance until our perceptions are renewed or awakened. Then that place of wisdom becomes a reality in your life, and Bone Woman becomes part of your inner council. She speaks a language you must learn. It is a language born from the will, and it helps you to restructure the way that you live.

"She speaks of the shadows that float behind each of us. I can see behind each and every one of you a newly formed shadow, and that shadow is made of fear—fear to be strong and beautiful, fear to be your wild power animal, predatory and awesome in the light of day. To name it, it is called your *shadow warrior,* born of your male shield, waiting to be used, because that's what he is. He is part of your celebration into the world of your new-found joy and stability and bone deep power."

Beth raised her hand, and taking a little crystal from her pocket, she said, "I hear your words deep inside me, and I realize for the first time that I have been in a place, in a state of intro-spection for years and years. I've hidden in my blood, like hiding in a forest without seeing the trees. The gateway of menopause marks a transition between my pulling back, moving into intro-spection, and healing myself, continually and always healing myself, trying to find the depths and the end of my self-wound. Now, I feel a true transition in the movement, or current, of my energy."

"Can you explain that further?" I asked. "Can you explain to all of us what that feels like, Beth?"

"I feel almost an explosion, I guess, as if the energy is imploded into me until there is no more room. And I fight with that energy now, instead of it being a flow of power into me as it has been for years. I suddenly realize that for years I have been introspecting, looking inside, always looking inside, and I would see an occasional reflection in the world, a mirror, of that intro-spection, but that's as far as it ever went. When I met Woman at the Edge of Two Worlds, I felt a shift in that energy, truly. And now, I'm not sure what's going to happen. I'm like a canoe going over the rapids. I pull the creative energy in and now it needs to be directed out in some kind of form. I dreamed of Bone Woman last night. She was gathering my bones in a big pile and re-sorting them as she put me back together."

Beth was silent for several minutes, as we all were, contem-plating Bone Woman and her place in our lives.

Mary placed a few kernels of corn, taken from a small medicine pouch hanging around her neck, into the circle. "My biggest problem with menopause is that I sense I am losing my power. I am relearning about my position within the sacred round of life. I realize that I approach life in a very sexual way. Woman at the Edge of Two Worlds said something very interest-ing to me. She said, 'It is time to grow up, my eternal child. You have difficulty with wise-blood because you're afraid to be wise. Whenever you get too close to success, you sabotage yourself. Now you have no choice, because wise-blood you are. You never had a childhood, so all your adult life you've wanted to play. And you still can, but now you must play as a wise adult. It is time, Mary. It is time.' Her words went to my core. She's right, you know. No wonder all my clients are afraid to grow up. It's because that's the lesson *I* need to learn. I love it and I hate it, but Woman at the Edge of Two Worlds changed my life. I'm not losing my sexuality; I'm losing my inability to take responsibility for my grown-up life."

Beth reached over and gave Mary a big hug.

Phyllis took a leaf that she had been holding in her hands, stroking with her fingers, and she laid it into the center of the circle. "May I speak?" she asked.

"Yes my sister," I said.

"I think I know that feeling as well. I experienced the same surge of energy when I met Woman at the Edge of Two Worlds, but when I felt that energy, I felt the gateway open inside myself, inside my shaman center, my will. As that gateway opened, I physically bled. I felt the blood coming down between my legs during that ceremony, and I felt that it was a sign, that it was a blessing. I did not feel as I always would have in my life, like I needed to run and cover up my blood. It was a statement almost of my femaleness giving one last drop of blood-essence to the sacred altar of my earlier life before it was held in the hands of Wise Woman forever more."

"Did it feel like a sacrifice of yourself to power in some way?" I asked her.

"Yes, Lynn. I felt as if it was the last sacrifice, a blood sacrifice, to the power of the Sacred Mother. And then it was through, as if my introspection was finished, as if finally, even though we are never completely healed in a lifetime, I felt a completion in a way. I felt that now instead of always pulling the energy in and imploding it and trying to build it, that it was built and that now I could explode into the world with my caring and my beauty and my strength. Ah!" she said. "And Lynn, that exploding into the world is the *shadow warrior,* is it not? It is the male shield held up, finally and at last, in the completion of the sacred dance of life, when the female implodes and the male explodes into existence—a manifestation of my own truth and life force. And the shield of my *shadow warrior,*" she said excitedly, "is blessed by Bone Woman. She awakens his shield, and his shield is made from her sacred bones."

"Ho!" we all said.

We passed the talking stick around the entire circle until it reached Olivia. I had asked her to join us before she journeyed south. Olivia had big tears in her brown eyes, and she said, "I want to share with you, my new sisters, something that is very important to me. As you might know, my womb was taken from me early, and I was thrown into menopause without being able to prepare for this feeling as you did. My body didn't subtly and slowly move into this process. It was suddenly initiated overnight by a surgeon's knife. When I met Woman at the Edge of Two Worlds, it was different for me. A great eagle from the east came down and took me in its talons and flew me over the world. Far below I could see everything—all the pain, all the struggle, and so much fear, like black thunder clouds over the earth. I felt that the earth was my womb, and my magical child must be given birth to heal the suffering. Like a giant egg, I gave birth to the idea for a new life for myself and my people. I felt sad at first in spite of her splendor and healing ways, sad that I was actually here at this gateway, because there's a part of me that did not want to be at this gateway, ever. I felt most whole in my life when I was giving birth to children, when I was full in my belly with a little one.

"But now I realize that I am giving birth in a different way, and I must work with my sisters. I will share with you my new dream." Olivia paused for a moment. "I know I must teach. I never ever felt secure enough as a woman of power to teach. This was always my problem. I gathered and I gathered, until my baskets were overflowing with knowledge, but never could I express into the world what I had learned. And I felt that explosion, too, my sisters. I felt that that is the true initiation of Woman at the Edge of Two Worlds. She allows and helps you to have the ability to change the flow of energy, and that energy is no longer inside the process of receiving, the process of giving an invitation, which is, to me, the power of woman. Now the alchemy is complete. She touched me with her fire and has shown me how to give back into the world what I am as a woman. And yes, Lynn, I understand that this giving back, which I have always done from the female aspect of myself, is now done through the *shadow warrior*. And I will dance with him around my council fires. I will wear the shawl of the *curandera*."

For several moments she closed her eyes as if searching for the words to explain the depth of her feeling. Then she opened her eyes and now they were clear. The sadness had vanished, and a great joy, a subtle light, surrounded her face.

"This is it," she said. "I never could understand how to go on. How could I go on into life, into a traditional life that I live, without my fertility? All of our ceremonies are about fertility and the regrowth and the death and rebirth of fertility in some way or another. Our life is about hunger, the hunger of our people and the hunger of my spirit. And somehow fertility is part of that. Growth and feeding. Do you understand?"

We all nodded, loving her deeply.

"I see now," Olivia said, the light shining down from the trees through the branches, the glow of sunlight like a halo around her head. "I feel for the first time that I can stand even higher than the men. Even though I understand the firstness of woman, in my village I never felt that. I felt always in the position of serving. I don't feel that any longer. Quite the contrary. I feel that I can implement change, that I am Changing Woman, and I can bring to my people a new vision, particularly to my women. *That* I can show them. I can help them initiate. I think that initiation is brought about with the *shadow warrior.* He will propel my ideas into being. The *shadow warrior* is part of me. He too carries my bones, my structure, my point of view, and I need to get to know him much better. Thank you sisters for listening."

We sat quietly together listening to the south wind in the trees.

Linda had been holding an acorn in her hand and she put it in her mouth. Then she tossed it into the center of the circle. "May I speak, sisters?"

"Ho!" we all said.

"There's a part of me that has been full of such hate and anger because of the inequities of life, not only toward my people, but toward all people. If there is anything more devastating on this planet, I can not imagine it to be anything other than human beings. But when I met Woman at the Edge of Two Worlds, something dissolved in me. I put that acorn in my mouth because it needed to feel my saliva. It wanted to be moist. I wanted to help it down its path. When I met Woman at the Edge of Two Worlds, I was the food for the saliva of the Great Mother. I wanted her to digest me, to take me in, change me and spit me out so that I no longer felt the anger and the hatred that is hidden inside me, that I'm even afraid to talk of, to speak of, because it sounds and is so ignorant. I found in our ceremony that there was a process of digestion. I, too, felt a shift in energy, and I felt that things I had learned, even as a child, things that were long forgotten came before my eyes in pictures. I saw them integrated for the first time ever. I think the reason is, and I didn't see it until this discussion, but I think the reason is that the energy shift that was created in that ceremony moved me somehow into balance."

Tears welled up in her eyes as she spoke. I watched the energy around her body move from red to a beautiful pink, which to me meant that she had balanced her mental thinking energy, that energy that is constantly trying to put things into a place of logic. I saw how that energy had balanced with her sexuality and her ability to physically express herself into the world.

"Yes, sisters, I feel deeply changed. Changing Woman I am. And yes, it is true, I have been introspecting also. I have been introspecting to the point that it is like a cow chewing her cud." We all laughed with her. "I have been ruminating over my problems and the problems of my people—what to do, what not to do—until I was almost paralyzed. And then menopause, and my husband seeming to reject me. I didn't know what to do. One night my hormones were going crazy and I had such a panic attack. I parked in front of the emergency hospital all night in case I needed help. But I've stopped fighting my body and the flashes. I ride them now like a horse and the fear is mostly gone. Most of the fear came from not knowing what was happening to me.

"Suddenly things are different. I know that I cannot be someone that I am not. I am a woman who has moved through the gateway of menopause, and you know something, for the first time, I am very proud. I am proud that I have made it. I didn't know whether I was going to live through this initiation. I felt that if I didn't die, that maybe I would kill myself, because I wasn't sure that I could face my life without my husband and without his desire of me. But suddenly there's a bigger issue. It is not outside me; it is inside me. That bigger issue is, maybe, what you called the *shadow warrior*, Lynn. Maybe that's what it is." She shook her head, and she said, "You know, I have felt this presence ever since our initiation in the cave and I couldn't find an understanding of that presence. I thought maybe it was my guardian. But no, it's not a guardian outside me, it's a guardian inside me. It is the male shield, isn't it, crying out, demanding attention, a warrior, strong. Like all of you, I have been presenting myself in the world through my female shield, and yet probably the more introspective side of me is this *shadow warrior*. No wonder my husband is confused about who I am."

"Yes," I said, "it confuses him. It confuses him only because when you become softer, you move into the male shield, not the female shield. Do you understand that?"

"I think I do," she said. "I realize that there is an anima and an animus in all of us, a female and a male. Many people don't like to hear that. When I would move out into the world in an expression of my political life and talk to my people, speak at rallies and write and manifest in the world my truth, I usually gave what I thought was, with the right side of my being, the male side. But that's not true, is it?"

"No," I said. "It isn't. I'm so full of love for you. I'm so happy for you, Linda, that you have seen this, because it will heal a great wound in you."

"Yes, I see. I am thankful to Woman at the Edge of Two Worlds for showing me this. She is the mirror."

"How did she show you this?" I asked.

"She showed me by being so balanced herself. She's a goddess. She is a strong goddess. She understands sacrifice and blood and war and hatred. It is a cauldron that forged her skeleton, and that skeleton was so evident to me. There is a killer in her if you attack her or those she loves. I could see that somewhere inside her there is true steel, that if you were ever to confront her in a warlike way, she would destroy you. She is kind and she is full of love, but she is a goddess, and a goddess knows how to defend herself. She would never lose her bones or her frame. A goddess knows how to make a statement in the cosmos about who she is. She never asks for approval, because if she asks for approval, she shows only weakness. She never doubts herself. She has worked for a long time, time beyond our perceptions. She has worked for the essence of truth. She has honed herself into a state of perfection, and I saw that. That can only happen when the male and the female energies are perfectly balanced. I realized that men-o-pause, just like you said, is a time to pause and consider, not only the goddess, but the maleness within you. That is part of the alchemy of this passage. It is the friction between the male and the female side that causes the fire that gives you the impetus to get through this and be strong, and that's what I feel. I feel the alchemy of the fire within, and it has changed me. I've learned to dance the fire instead of hiding inside myself. Without menopause I never would have learned that. That's what I'm going to do now with my husband. And I think by helping my husband understand this—"

"Perhaps you will never have to say anything," I said, interrupting her. "Just your being the way you are now is such a departure from the woman I first knew. Maybe by your moving he will have to move," I said.

"Yes, I think that is correct, and I feel it. As I say it to all of you, the moment I returned from that ceremony, my husband seemed to give up something that he thought he needed in terms of our relationship. He just gave it away, and as he gave it away, the passion returned to our marriage."

"I have to ask you one question, Linda. What was it that he gave away?"

She looked slowly down to the ground and traced a circle into the earth with her finger. Then she looked at all of us, and she said, "He gave up a myth."

"What was that myth?" I asked.

"It was his myth, not mine, of who I needed to be to please him. And somehow he just gave that away. I think if myths are needed in someone's life, that's okay. He has not raised this to me yet, but I think he made up a new myth. And that's okay, because it works. Whatever that myth is, he seems to no longer need me to have children. When he gave that up and realized that there was something even better behind that threat, he returned to a state of health and so did our marriage."

"Ho," we all said in unison.

I turned to Beth. "Beth, I have one question for you," I said. Beth sat up straight and took a last sip of iced tea. "Do you feel complete with Woman at the Edge of Two Worlds and with how you've grown from this experience?"

Beth in her usual thoughtful way sat back and placed on her lap a small pillow that she had brought to work needlepoint on as we talked through the afternoon. "I have, I think, taken off my rose-colored glasses," she said. "I have always been a bit of a Pollyanna. I have always been so innocent and naive." We all giggled with her because it was so true. "Something about meeting with Woman at the Edge of Two Worlds brought me at least a step closer to reality. I don't see the world in the same way, and I'm not quite sure why."

"Try to explain that," I said.

"Well, I am younger than you, all of you, and yet I can never have children. It is true, I didn't know whether or not I wanted to live. I couldn't imagine not having a family. Now I feel like the world is my family. I feel that you, sisters, are my family. I feel, in a sense, like I am giving birth to myself. I had taken care of my mother for such a long time before she died, and I was very close to her. When she died, I felt as if, like you, Lynn, when your mother passed on, as if a part of me went with her. Yet, when I was walking in a field after we had met with Woman at the Edge of Two Worlds, I had a vision that I was walking with my power animal, and I felt as if that power animal were as real as the trees that surrounded me. The vision that I saw was that my mother had given birth to me, that there was a time when I lived inside her belly. Now, through her death process, the circle is complete."

"How is that?" I asked.

"It is complete because now my mother lives inside me, like you said, and through this magic, I will be giving birth to her every day. I will be manifesting a very powerful female shield. I do not yet understand the male shield counterpart, the *shadow warrior*. That is something that I have to work with. But I see that shield now, and I feel that very strongly inside me waiting for me to have the strength to express it. That's what the fire has done for me. I make things with the fire like a blacksmith bends iron. Sometimes when hot flashes come, I see them in colors, and I allow myself to envision my dreams coming true. I use the heat to propel visualizations into being. As a result my legs don't seem to ache anymore, as they had been doing at night, and I'm metabolizing calcium much better. I'm restructuring my life with Bone Woman. When Woman at the Edge of Two Worlds came to me, Bone Woman came as well. She told me that the secret to my life was held in my bones and that to live anew, I must heal them. The loss of calcium was a sign, a plea for help from my bones to pay attention to what I was losing. My legs hurt. I didn't have a leg to stand on. Like that day in the meadow, Lynn, I have to take courage like the egret and fly away to my highest dream. To fly, I need my *shadow warrior*, my power mate. I know that now, and as I speak, I feel him strongly. It's not sexual, but a wild instinct for wholeness, an alchemy of blending that is brewing inside in the cauldron of my soul."

We picked up our drums and played the heartbeat of Mother Earth for some time. Then we looked at each other in silence, and every one of us felt supported in the knowledge that we all cared deeply about the continued evolution and success of each other's lives. We were bonded, sisters in spirit. I gave them sweet-grass that I had braided and dried for them, and we blessed each other in parting.

25

CHANGING WOMAN GATEWAY

A few weeks later I went north to be with my teachers. Ruby, Agnes, and I were sitting on the porch of Agnes's cabin. I was sitting on the old floor boards, running my fingers over the pine grain in the wood and tracing the circumference of an old knothole. I was ringing with life and well being. There was a silence between us, a respectful silence as we each honored the presence of the others and our need to be quiet. I looked out at the aurora borealis filling the sky with pulsating light, orange, pink, and golden flashes, as if the world were under siege somewhere in the far distance. But at this moment the magnificent lights that I had seen so often felt different to me. They seemed more gentle somehow, for a fleeting moment, as if the spirits of all of my apprentices were represented there in a light show in the sky. I saw the faces of all of them, so full of life and vibrancy, and each and every one of them radiating unique and extraordinary colors into the universe.

I turned to Agnes, who had been watching me for some time, and I asked, "Agnes, you have never told me about your passage through the Changing Woman gateway. You have never told me of your meeting with Woman at the Edge of Two Worlds."

Agnes looked fleetingly toward Ruby and then looked back at

me with a large smile, her perfect white teeth flashing in the evening light. "Ruby and I went through the initiation together," Agnes said.

"You did?" I was full of wonderment. I suddenly realized there was a whole time frame of their lives that I knew nothing about. I was eager to hear the story. "Agnes, tell me about it. There is so much that I don't know about your life, so much that I will never be able to share."

"But my daughter," Agnes said, suddenly very gentle, putting her hand on my shoulder, "you experience the result of all of my lifetimes, all of what I have become, just sitting here now in this old rocking chair. I am full for our knowledge and wisdom together, my daughter. I am full of love."

Tears almost leapt out of my eyes, I was so touched by the depth of emotion in her voice.

"Humph," Ruby said. "It took you long enough, Little Wolf, to ask about us. Took you long enough to wonder what *our* experience was."

I faced Ruby almost stunned. I caught my breath as I fought back the tears. "Surely I have asked something about your passage," I said.

Agnes with a smile and Ruby with an expression of indignity stared at me.

"Well, then now's the time," I said finally, having to laugh as they laughed with me.

It was always Ruby's position in my life with them to pull me back to reality, back to a center of truth. Whenever I lost myself in a moment, lost myself in confusion, or any other emotion, Ruby was there, pulling me back to center. Usually she behaved as the sacred clown, prodding me, testing me, even kicking me verbally sometimes when it was needed, to move me back, to pull my mind away from the illusions of conscious life and move me back into touch with my intuition and my place of power. Oftentimes, I have heard people say that they either love Ruby in my books or they really don't like her a lot, or they've never been able to relate to Ruby, never have understood her and my relationship with her. But mostly I have found that my readers have been deeply touched by her as I have been. She is the one that I am most afraid of. Yet she is the one who is the benefactor of my spirit. Agnes is my teacher, but together they have woven this tapestry that I have called my path—together. Very carefully and with great reverence for the mysteries of power in the universe, they have taught me about the ancient power of woman. It is Ruby who brings in the humor and the passion and my anger. She is the one who helps me understand the meaning of love and awakens my will with her words. Her timing is impeccable.

I sat back on the porch as Agnes lifted her face toward the sky, her eyes closed. She placed her hands in her lap. "Ruby and I went through the initiation with Woman at the Edge of Two Worlds when we were much older than you," she said, opening her eyes and tilting her head slightly.

She had a red Navajo blanket over her lap, keeping her legs warm. She was wearing three medicine bags, sewn with red trade beads and very old. Her face at this moment, instead of being deeply furrowed and lined with the imprint of time and life, seemed younger, as if with her words her physical body moved back in history to an event she was thinking of, the event of menopause.

"We were in our middle fifties," Agnes said. "As you know, Little Wolf, I had been through a lot of tragedy. My husband was killed in a logging accident not long after our daughter crawled out of our hut in the far north during a blizzard and was taken by our sled dogs. Because of that tragedy, and this is a story that you know well, but it is part of the puzzle, part of the shield that I speak of, I did not want to live after I lost my family. I wanted only to sleep an eternal sleep. When I found it impossible to take my own life, I went in search of a teacher. When I found the Sisterhood, I became whole again, but because of that extraordinary grief, because it took me a long time to come to my power, for some reason, my moon stayed with me. Perhaps to cleanse me every month. Perhaps to purify what I was putting my body through. I do not know. But I could not marry again. I had been with who I felt was my spirit mate in this lifetime. It was not until I met the women of the Sisterhood of the Shields that I understood why things happen in life. I understood that there is a reason for all of the pain and the struggle and the difficulty that we have all lived through.

"When I met Ruby—Ruby, who had been raped and whose eyes had been blinded by the compasses of the white surveyors— she had lost her man at that time. She had lost her way, and the great Sautox medicine man in the north moved into her body and soul and healed her with the forces of lightning and the deer spirits. He healed her so that she sees now better than you or I. But in that healing she, too, found her way as a great healer and a great teacher. Ruby is a *heyoka* woman, a backwards woman. She falls back into the arms of the Great Spirit with absolute trust and inspires that wisdom in all of us. Ruby knows how to laugh. Ruby knows the absurdity of it all, particularly the absurdity of taking ourselves too seriously. Whenever you take yourself too seriously, Black Wolf, that is when Ruby comes to visit you, is that not so?"

I nodded my head, understanding deeply the knowledge that she was speaking of, and I had the scars to prove it, dear scars that I would not trade for anything. I looked at Ruby sitting still as a post in her chair, her eyes looking toward the horizon, her milky blue eyes of no sight and great vision.

"We were initiated together, just as you and Olivia were, by the Sisterhood of the Shields. One day I sat on the moss by the river and I let the blood of my body, of my femaleness, of my essence, flow into that moss as a gift back to Mother Earth. I remember that day so well. In those times we went to the moon lodge, all of us that bled together, because when we lived in camp together, all of the women bled together as well, and we welcomed the moon lodge. It was not as people have often thought, that women in their moon are dirty and need to be off by themselves until it's over with, that somehow it's a curse. Oh, no. It was a time of sharing, of laughter, that we looked forward to every month. It is something that people in your society have missed completely, and that brings me great sadness, because right there," Agnes said, "you lose the rhythm of mother nature. You lose the understanding of the power of the moon and the tides. You lose your relationship with the source of power, and woman is the source of power, although it seems to have been long forgotten. There is even a reason for that."

Ruby and Agnes giggled together like children. I sat staring at them in wonderment, trying to understand and see in my mind's eye a world that I would never know. It was because of them that I was inspired to write about shamanism and personal power.

Ruby shook her head and looked at me with a wink, and said, "You teach and write about the heart and the spirit of woman."

I blinked, looking at her, thinking, How is it they know every thought in my mind? Suddenly, Agnes and Ruby laughed, slapping their thighs, rocking back and forth. I laughed with them. What else was there to do but laugh? Certainly I had never learned from anyone else I had ever met a better understanding for the pulse of nature that we can all feel if we simply open our hearts and our senses. Shamanism is a training about something that we cannot see or touch. It involves the touching of energy; it involves that instinctual feminine part of our consciousness that so much of so called civilized life has denied.

"It was a joyous time," Agnes went on, "when we experienced our last flow together, both of us sitting on that moss by the river together. Both of us knew that it was our last time in the moon lodge, and the next day both of us lost our flow forever."

"But it was time," Ruby chimed in. "It was time we moved through the gateway. It was time that we held up our sacred prayer sticks to the moon. It was time that we met you, my daughter."

My head swiveled around to look at Ruby. "What do you mean?"

"It was then that we were told of your coming," Agnes said, smiling.

"I don't understand," I said.

"There was a legend about a white woman coming to us. It was told to both of us by Woman at the Edge of Two Worlds during our initiation. That legend also spoke of the marriage basket, our sacred basket that was woven by the dreams of all women, our ceremonial basket. It was said in legend that a priest would come to us and that he would throw down his vestments and would want to learn about the world of power and would apprentice himself to Agnes Whistling Elk; that this man was an evil man. He could not integrate his female nature with his male shield, and he would fall away from the teachings. In his anger and frustration, he would steal the marriage basket, and of course, that man was Red Dog. It was told then that a white woman would come asking for teaching and that she would be the one to take back the marriage basket and return it to the Sacred Dreamers."

I looked into both of their faces, never having heard this legend before exactly as they were telling me.

"It was then," Agnes went on, "that we knew that our life would become more public, that even though the world would never see us as we are, that the Sisterhood of the Shields would become known to other cultures around the world and that this white woman would move out into the world as one of our sisters, speaking of our truth and our knowledge that we had kept secret for so long. We also saw in the ceremonial fires, as we were being initiated, the torment in the world and the ecology so out of balance because of the misuse of money and the materialistic focus of our societies. We saw our great Mother Earth in danger of wobbling off and dying. It was then that we understood why we must go through the gateway at that time, that we had to hold up our shields and our sacred drums and take up the heartbeat of Mother Earth to restore her to health and balance.

"So you see, my daughter, it is also time for you. It is time for you to hold up the sacred drums, the sacred shields of our Sisterhood and walk Mother Earth, speaking of our truth and our love for this great earth mother that we need to heal."

Ruby looked at me and held out her hands. I felt her fingers with mine and the strength of her grip.

"It is time, my daughter. It is near dark, the time when the world changes and the mysteries of power walk the crossroads of the earth. Come, join us in ceremony."

POSTSCRIPT

Events that occur in your life—like marriage or death, the birth of a child, menopause—are mirrors that help you to grow, if you look at the events in that way. To grow with an experience, like menopause, that is truly out of your control, you need to look at all aspects of how you are reacting to the event. In other words, you need to go to your doctor, go to an endrocrinologist as well as a gynecologist. Understand the imbalances that are being created in your body. Understand as fully as you can a medical event that doesn't seem to have been very well researched. Understand as well as you can, not only from regular doctors, but also from homeopaths, about what happens when hormones grow into a state of imbalance. What does it mean when progesterone is lower than estrogen or visa versa? What about testosterone? How does that affect you emotionally and energetically? A lot of people will not readily give you those answers, but you can create your own study when you know what the facts are in terms of your own blood tests and biology. If a doctor or clinician places an illegible graph under your nose, don't rest until you fully understand it. I learned that I had to be persistant to get answers from many doctors who were too busy to take the time to explain facts so that I understood them. Perhaps by working with a teacher or a doctor or experienced homeopaths, acupressurists and acupuncturists, you can come to your own educated conclusions, and you can learn deeply from this research. It is all part of your study as a woman of power.

For more than a decade, I've been describing my learning and my path. It has been a joy to do this. In continuing my journey, I would be grateful if you would share your insights with me.

Please write me at:

Lynn Andrews
2934 ½ Beverly Glen Circle
Box 378
Los Angeles, CA 90077

Please send me your name and address so I can share any new information with you.

In Spirit,